"Sean McDowell has a gift for taking tou down to earth in practical ways that mak great help to all of you guys who are stru hardest questions!"

William Lane Craig
Research Professor of Philosophy, Talbot School of Theology

"It is completely evident that Sean McDowell understands the hearts and culture of today's youth. Sean offers truths that are relevant and a benefit to students everywhere."

Shaun Blakeney
Saddleback Church, High School Pastor

"No book is more to the point of the moral needs of today's teens and parents than this clear, concise, and commendable text by Sean McDowell."

Norman Geisler
Former President and co-founder, Southern Evangelical Seminary;
Author of over 50 books on ethics and apologetics

"*Ethix* is a powerful resource for young people who want to be transformed, passionate followers of Jesus Christ and know how to answer a world that mocks the standards of the Bible."

Ron Luce
President, Teen Mania Ministries

"Sean McDowell has written a masterful book on ethics for young Christians. I wish every teenager in my church would read, study, and heed its wisdom."

James W. Sire
Author of *The Universe Next Door*

"*Ethix* is a much-needed book. Young people need to be challenged today to use their minds and to think about the most important issues in life. Sean has done just that."

J. P. Moreland
Distinguished Professor of Philosophy, Talbot School of Theology,
Biola University, and Coauthor of *The Lost Virtue of Happiness*

"Sean McDowell has a tremendous skill in relating truth to students. *Ethix* is a must-read for every young person in a day when teenagers need clarity in what to believe and not to believe."

Chuck Klein
National Director, Student Venture, Campus Crusade for Christ

"Learning to think with a Christian mind is one of our great tasks. This is especially true in the area of what's right and what's wrong. I am thankful for *Ethix*. Highly recommended!"

David A. Noebel
President, Summit Ministries; Author, *Understanding the Times*

"Sean McDowell is part of a generation of young Christian thinkers who are fast becoming leaders in equipping the church in mastering the intellectual power of the Christian tradition."

Francis J. Beckwith
Associate Director, J. M. Dawson Institute of Church-State Studies; Associate Professor of Church-State Studies, Baylor University

"The world has devalued truth, yet truth has consequences. *Ethix* provides you with a clear road map through the dangerous terrain of the modern world. Sean McDowell helps you make sure you know how to make the right decision."

Kerby Anderson
National Director, Probe Ministries; Author, *Christian Ethics in Plain Language*

"While churches all over the country are lowering the bar for young people, Sean McDowell is raising it. In *Ethix* he has given his generation of Christians both map and compass to navigate this chaotic "whatever" culture."

Gregory Koukl
President, Stand to Reason; Coauthor, *Relativism: Feet Firmly Planted in Thin Air*

"Sean McDowell has given students a wonderful start in building a biblical worldview. Sean makes theological truth practical. *Ethix* is a must-read for students, parents, and youth workers."

Jim Burns, Ph.D.
President, HomeWord

"There's a new voice bringing clarity and direction in the twenty-first century. His name is Sean McDowell. His book *Ethix* brings reasoned guidance and solid answers for today's youth. Every parent, youth pastor, middle-schooler, and high-school student needs to read this engaging book!"

Mike Licona
Director of Apologetics Evangelism, North American Mission Board

"*Ethix* will equip you to make right decisions in a world that has abandoned truth."

Greg Stier
President, Dare 2 Share Ministries

"*Ethix* is a profoundly important book for helping this generation establish anchor points for their life and creates a basis for the decisions they are making. Sean McDowell tells the truth about truth."

Monty Hipp
President, the C4 Group

"In a world of moral relativism, students need to know how to think clearly and biblically about the tough issues in life. Sean McDowell takes a fresh and captivating approach to answering these most difficult questions. I highly commend it to you."

Dr. Dann Spader
Founder, Sonlife Ministries; President, Global Youth Initiative

BEING BOLD IN A WHATEVER WORLD

SEAN MCDOWELL

NASHVILLE TENNESSEE

Printed in the United States of America

ISBN: 978-0-8054-4519-0

Published by B&H Publishing Group
Nashville, Tennessee

Dewey Decimal Classification: 241
Subject Headings: CHRISTIAN ETHICS \ YOUTH—ETHICS
CHRISTIAN LIFE

Passages that include italicized text indicate McDowell's emphasis.

08 09 10 11 12 17 16 15 14 13 12 11 10 9 8 7 6 5

To my wife Stephanie,
a true example of someone who
lives boldly for what she believes.

CONTENTS

Acknowledgments

The first person I would like to thank is **my father Josh**. No son could be more proud of the way a father boldly models his convictions. I appreciate your help, feedback, and insights on this project. And thank you to my mother Dottie for her edits and encouragement throughout the entire process.

Thanks **to Brannon Howse**, president of Worldview Weekends, for introducing me to the fine people at Broadman & Holman and for his guidance during the writing process.

I am grateful to all of **my personal editors** who gave me such insightful feedback, including **Brett Kunkle, Carlos Delgado, Stephen Wagner**, and the **editors from Broadman & Holman.**

Thank you to the entire team at B & H, and especially **David Shepherd, Lisa Parnell, and Stephanie Huffman**. I consider it a privilege to be part of the TQ line of resources, which is a vitally important contribution to help our young people stand up boldly for the Christian faith.

Thank you to **my Lord and Savior, Jesus Christ.** You are truly the perfect example of love and boldness in action. I pray that this book, and my life, will play one piece in building your kingdom.

Standing Up for What Is Right

PURPOSE

To understand the importance of making right choices for a meaningful and happy life

In this chapter you will learn

- What it takes to have a life of happiness rather than a life of emptiness
- Four reasons why right choices are so important
- Helpful ideas for taking a stand for what is right

Jana had never imagined she would be facing the decision that was before her today. As a former member of a high school youth group, she had learned much about making right choices and honoring God in her daily life, but this seemed to be beyond anything she had been tested with before. *How can I possibly do the right thing,* she wondered, *when my college psychology professor has assigned me to watch four one-hour periods of X-rated pornographic films and write a personal review as part of my grade?* Without this assignment Jana's grade would suffer greatly, but she also knew that God's desire was for her to be sexually pure. What *should* she do?

Michael's history teacher gave an essay assignment with the freedom to choose any historical person. As a Christian, Michael decided to write on the life of Jesus of Nazareth. When he turned in his proposal, his teacher adamantly objected, even though others in the class were writing on religious figures. He tried to reason with her, but she refused to budge. How should he respond? Should he stand up and be bold for his faith?

After going out with Tim for six months, Jennifer began to feel that she was falling in love with him. He was sensitive, caring, and so much fun. Her dad paid little attention to her, and she desperately wanted genuine affection. They had set physical boundaries before, but now they were feeling so close to each other they began to wonder, *If we are truly in love, how can it* not *be right for us to have sex?* Is it OK, because they are in love and may end up getting married some day, for them to have sex? Is it really that big of a deal? Won't God forgive them anyway?

What would you do if you were in any of the above situations? Does it really matter what choices Jana, Michael, and Jennifer make? Can the choices you make as a young person have an effect on your future as an adult? And how can you take a stand for what is right when there are so many odds against you? In Plato's *Republic,* Socrates says, "We are discussing no small matter here, but how we ought to live." His point is simple—the most important question we ask in life is not related to our career, or where we live, or even to where we go to college. The most important question relates to the issue of *how* we live our lives—what, or whom, do we live for?

Every day you face moral choices: Should I respect my parents? Should I cheat on my upcoming exam? How far should I go with my boyfriend or girlfriend? Should I see a certain movie? You will face moral dilemmas that will cause you to make difficult decisions. How you respond to these choices determines who you are right now and, in turn, shapes who you become. The purpose of this book is to equip you to think through some of today's most pressing moral issues so you can take a stand for what is right and be the type of person God wants you to be.

HAPPINESS OR EMPTINESS?

In the film *XXX,* Vin Diesel plays Xander Cage, a notorious underground thrill-seeker whom until now the law has deemed untouchable. But, because he has three strikes against him and does not want to go to prison, Cage is forced to accept a special underground assignment involving the Russian mafia. Through a series of high-flying stunts that border on the impossible (and a whole lot of attitude), Cage fulfills his special government assignment and is set free.

Clearly, young adults are the target audience of *XXX*. Shortly after the release of the movie, Diesel was interviewed by *Entertainment Weekly*. When asked about his role in the movie, he said, "We are totally reinventing the spy film for a new generation. *XXX* is not Austin Powers; this is not a spoof—it's a real spy film. But it is not James Bond. It's totally different. It's urban and multiethnic. It's got X games, tattoos, and body-piercing. There is a whole new attitude in this movie. We've come up with a different kind of hero—a nihilist, an anti-hero, a guy who doesn't give a —— about anything but his own thrills."

In other words, *the hero for today is supposed to be the person who does not care about values and only lives for the thrill of the moment.* If Diesel were confronted with the dilemmas I presented above, he might say, "Hey, just do what feels good. Live for the thrill of the moment, and don't worry about anyone or anything else."

Although it may be appealing for some to live for the thrill of the moment, if you follow Diesel's advice you ultimately will end up living a hollow life. Imagine marrying a man or woman with this philosophy. As soon as you stopped giving him or her thrills, your husband or wife would be out the door. You certainly would not have a committed relationship. In Proverbs 14:12, Solomon warns, "There is a way which seems right to a man, but its end is the way of death." Not only are there often painful consequences for ignoring truth, but a person who seeks meaning solely from thrills is destined to be empty.

Interestingly, recent studies indicate that, for more than any other generation in history, this has come true for your generation. Young people today are buying into Vin Diesel's view of life and, as a result, are more depressed than any previous generation. Why is this so? Why do so many young people today lack a sense of purpose and meaning in their lives? The simple reason is that many young people have bought into the false view of happiness promoted by our culture. So many youth today think their lives will have meaning *only* if they can fill them up with thrills or with material goods. But, despite what Vin Diesel might claim, this view only leads to emptiness.

Just think about it for a moment. What will a night of binge drinking bring you? At first it may seem so exciting, so new. But let's ask the questions most people want to ignore: *Will it truly make you feel good?* The thrill might last for a fleeting moment but not for the long run. What will happen when you are done with the thrill? Will it give you a sense of belonging? In all likelihood you will be depressed, lonely, and in search of something else to fill you up. So many people live their entire lives trying to find happiness and meaning in a place it simply can't be found. Are you willing to entertain another possibility?

IS THERE ANOTHER WAY?

Two thousand years ago Jesus gave his followers a sermon about the most important things in life. He summed up the core of his message when he said, "But seek first the kingdom of God and His righteousness, and all these things will be provided for you" (Matt. 6:33 HCSB). In other words, the most important thing for us to focus on is *not* our own thrills or possessions, but to *focus first on building God's kingdom and living rightly*. And amazingly, when we forget about our own thrills and focus on making the lives of other people better, we end up living a fulfilled and meaningful life.

Consider some truths about young people who believe in God that were pointed out in *Time* magazine's annual happiness issue:

- Teen believers are generally less stressed and happier than nonbelievers.
- Teen believers are less depressed, less anxious, and less suicidal than nonreligious people.
- Teens who attend services, read the Bible, pray, and help other people are less alone, less misunderstood, and more cared for than their nonreligious peers.[1]

Happiness is not found when we seek thrills at the expense of making right choices. Happiness is when we become virtuous people committed to building God's kingdom. Only when we stop focusing so selfishly on ourselves and begin caring about other people will we find true meaning in life. You see, this is the paradox of the Christian life—you only truly find your place in life when you stop focusing solely on yourself! This is why Jesus said, "If anyone wants to be first, he must be last of all and servant of all" (Mark 9:35). Similarly, former President Jimmy Carter gave the following advice to young people: "All of us wonder about our real purpose in life. For a few, this question can become a profound source of anxiety. When we have inner turmoil that needs healing, uncertainty about the meaning of life can grow into an obsession with self-pity or depression. For many people the best solution is to think of something we can do for someone else. . . . No matter what we seek in life, we are more likely to find it if we are not self-centered but concentrate on *something* or *someone* outside ourselves."[2]

FOUR REASONS WHY RIGHT CHOICES ARE SO IMPORTANT

I. Right Choices Build Character

One of my mentors shared the following truth with me when I was younger: "The choices you make today determine the person you will become tomorrow." In other words, our daily choices build the foundation of our character, which is who we *truly* are in our innermost being. My dad once put it to me this way: "Sow a thought, reap an act; sow an act, reap a habit; sow a habit, reap a character; sow a character, reap a destiny." It is humbling to realize that the choices we make *even today* help shape our futures. In fact, at any moment in our lives our ability to make good choices is influenced by our previous choices. Let me explain.

Have you ever told a lie? After you told that lie, was it easier or harder to tell another lie the next time? I think you will admit, if you are being honest, that the second time was much easier than the first. Now have you ever stood up for what is right? If you have, you realize that it becomes easier to do the right thing the more often you do it. Do you treat people with respect? Do you protect your mind by being cautious about the images you put in front of your eyes? Do you submit to authority? Making right choices is so important because it is the process through which we mold our character.

This is a truth that the biblical story of Joseph illustrates well. Since Jacob favored Joseph over all the twelve brothers, the other eleven brothers sold Joseph to an Egyptian slave-trader. Alone in a foreign land, Joseph became a slave in the hands of Potiphar, a prominent court official in Egypt. Because of Joseph's faithfulness and hard work Potiphar made Joseph overseer not only of his house but of all he owned.

Soon, though, Joseph faced the test of a lifetime. Potiphar's wife—no doubt a beautiful woman—tried to seduce Joseph into having sex with her. Just think of all the excuses Joseph could have given to justify sleeping with her: "No one will ever know"; "I've been so lonely here in Egypt away from my family"; "Nobody will get hurt." But Joseph refused to betray his master and, ultimately, his God.

Joseph consistently made right choices, even when he was young. What gave Joseph the strength to make the right decision when there were so many reasons to give in? For one thing, Joseph had committed himself to following God, regardless of his surrounding circumstances. Even though he was sent as a slave to a foreign land, and then thrown in prison, he still determined not to betray his God. His commitment to doing right built a foundation in his life that ultimately led to his showing kindness to and providing for his brothers—the very people who had betrayed him!

2. Right Choices Protect Us

My dad once shared a story with me about a young man named Greg. He lived right down the street from a family with a concrete swimming pool in their yard. Although Greg barely knew the people and had never used their pool, he figured it wouldn't be a big deal. Late one evening he and his girlfriend snuck into their back yard, climbed the fence, and entered the pool area to go for a swim. They ignored the signs that read "Do not swim."

Greg took off his shoes, jumped on the ladder and, while his girlfriend was still removing her shoes and socks, dove off the end of the diving board.

He heard the scream from his girlfriend the moment before he lost consciousness. The water from the pool had been drained for painting. Greg's dive ended with a shallow splash of water and a sickening crunch of bones. Greg was paralyzed from the neck down for the rest of his life.

Greg completely ignored the protective fence put up by his neighbors. He supposed it was there only to keep him and his girlfriend from having fun. In truth, the fence was designed to protect him. His indifference to the boundary cost him his ability to walk again. Similarly, when we ignore God's moral boundaries, *which God has put in place for our benefit*, the cost can be devastating. Consider the consequences for the following choices:

- **Pre-marital Sex:** About 3 million teenagers contract an STD every year.[3] Pre-marital sex also can lead to guilt, pregnancy, and relational conflict.
- **Abortion:** Young women who have abortions are one-third more likely to develop breast cancer.[4] Women who have had abortions are 30 percent more likely to suffer from symptoms such as anxiety, irri-

tability, fatigue, and difficulty in sleeping.[5]

- **Homosexuality:** Three out of four homosexual men will get an STD during their lifetime.[6]
- **Lying:** All healthy relationships are built on trust. When we lie we lose the trust of loved ones and taint our reputation.

God's moral rules are not designed to steal our fun, but to protect us from harm and pain. And not only do God's guidelines protect us from harm, they provide for us immeasurable blessings.

3. Right Choices Provide for Us

At an amusement park when I was younger, I tried to make my way through a life-sized maze. Without much of a sense of direction, I wandered back and forth from one dead end to another. Looking up at my dad, who was watching me navigate my journey from above, I remember wishing I had his enlightened perspective. *It would be easy*, I thought, *if I could just see the whole maze*.

God has a vantage point for our lives much like my dad did for the maze. God can see through the moral maze of life much better than we can, and his commands are designed to keep us from heading toward dead ends. When God says to remain pure or to be honest or to respect life, he is not trying to ruin our fun; rather, he wants to guide us through the moral maze of life so that we can experience his best. This is why the author of Deuteronomy writes, "Now, Israel, what does the LORD your God require from you, but to fear the LORD your God, to walk in all His ways and love Him, and to serve the LORD your God with all your heart and with all your soul, and to keep the LORD'S commandments and His statutes which I am commanding you today *for your good?"* (10:12–13).

As a teenager I made a decision that I was going to wait to have sex within the loving commitment of marriage. While there were many temptations and times it would have been easy to give in, I thank God that he gave me the strength to trust him. My wife and I both entered marriage as virgins, and we have never had the slightest shadow of regret or fear over what we were bringing into the marriage bed. We are protected from sexually transmitted diseases, guilt, and the strain of comparison with past lovers. And there are also incredible benefits. We have a real trust in our marriage, a genuine intimacy that, had we not made right choices when we were younger, would have been difficult to achieve. The honest, intimate relationship I now experience with my wife is an example of the provision that results from moral choices.

Jeremiah 29:11 says, "'For I know the plans I have for you,' says the LORD. 'They are plans for good and not for disaster, to give you a future and a hope'" (NLT). God truly wants us to have fulfilled and meaningful lives. He wants to bless us in ways that right now are unimaginable. In order to experience God's blessings, we need to trust him every day with our choices.

4. Right Choices Make Us Examples to Our Peers

Not only do right choices protect and provide for us, they make us examples to our peers. When I was a senior in high school I received a phone call I will *never* forget. Tim, a junior at my school, called me up personally to ask me a question about an incident we were both involved in at school that day. The incident involved a colorful leather hat that I had bought in Mexico (and, believe it or not, I wore it almost every day). Yet one day, to my chagrin, my hat was missing. A few days later, Tim showed up wearing the *exact* same hat. While I really didn't know Tim, I knew he was a troubled kid. Because it seemed like too much of a coincidence, I approached him and asked for my hat back. He swore that it was his hat, so I chose to believe him and not push it any further.

That night Tim called to ask me a simple question. "Why," he said, "did you treat me with such kindness?" To be honest, I was *shocked* to hear him say that. He seemed like such a "hard" kid. Why would he care what I said or thought? But what really broke my heart was that I didn't have the courage to share my faith with him. He had noticed something different about me, but I passed up an opportunity to share Jesus with him for fear of being rejected or made fun of. One year after I graduated from high school, his older brother, who was in my class, committed suicide. I have so often looked back at that incident in my life and wondered if I could have helped prevent this tragedy. If they had known the powerful love of Jesus, their lives might have been very different.

This incident taught me a powerful lesson—that people really do notice how we live our lives. Even the "hardest" people are searching for belonging, and many times they are watching what choices we make. I just wish I had been bold enough to reach out to him, even if he had made fun of me. We are supposed to set the example for other people because that is exactly what God has done for us.

"Follow God's example in everything you do, because you are his dear children. Live a life filled with love for others, following the example of Christ, who loved you and gave himself as a sacrifice to take away your sins" (Eph. 5:1–2 NLT). People may not always notice, but many times they will.

TAKING A STAND FOR WHAT IS RIGHT

Remember Jana from the beginning of the chapter? Her teacher said to her, "You either watch the pornographic films or I will dock you a full grade." Should she compromise her grade or compromise her morals? Could there be another way? After much prayer, thought, and counsel, she came up with an idea. She decided to make a proposal to her teacher. She proposed that he allow her to write a paper on why she should not have to do the assignment. If he accepted it, then she would be excused. Although the teacher thought he would never accept the paper, he decided to agree to the proposal anyway.

After much research and thought, Jana wrote a four-page paper on why, as a believer and follower of Christ, she should not watch X-rated pornography. Can you guess what happened? Not only did the teacher accept her paper, but her paper so articulately illustrated her point of view that he had her come up in front of the entire class and read her findings on the day they were set to watch the pornographic films. He then told the class that anyone who wanted to be excused from the assignment could be excused as well without it adversely affecting their grade. Nearly half the class—both Christian and non-Christian students—stood up and walked out of the room! This shows the power of one person with convictions standing up for what is right. Are you up for the challenge?

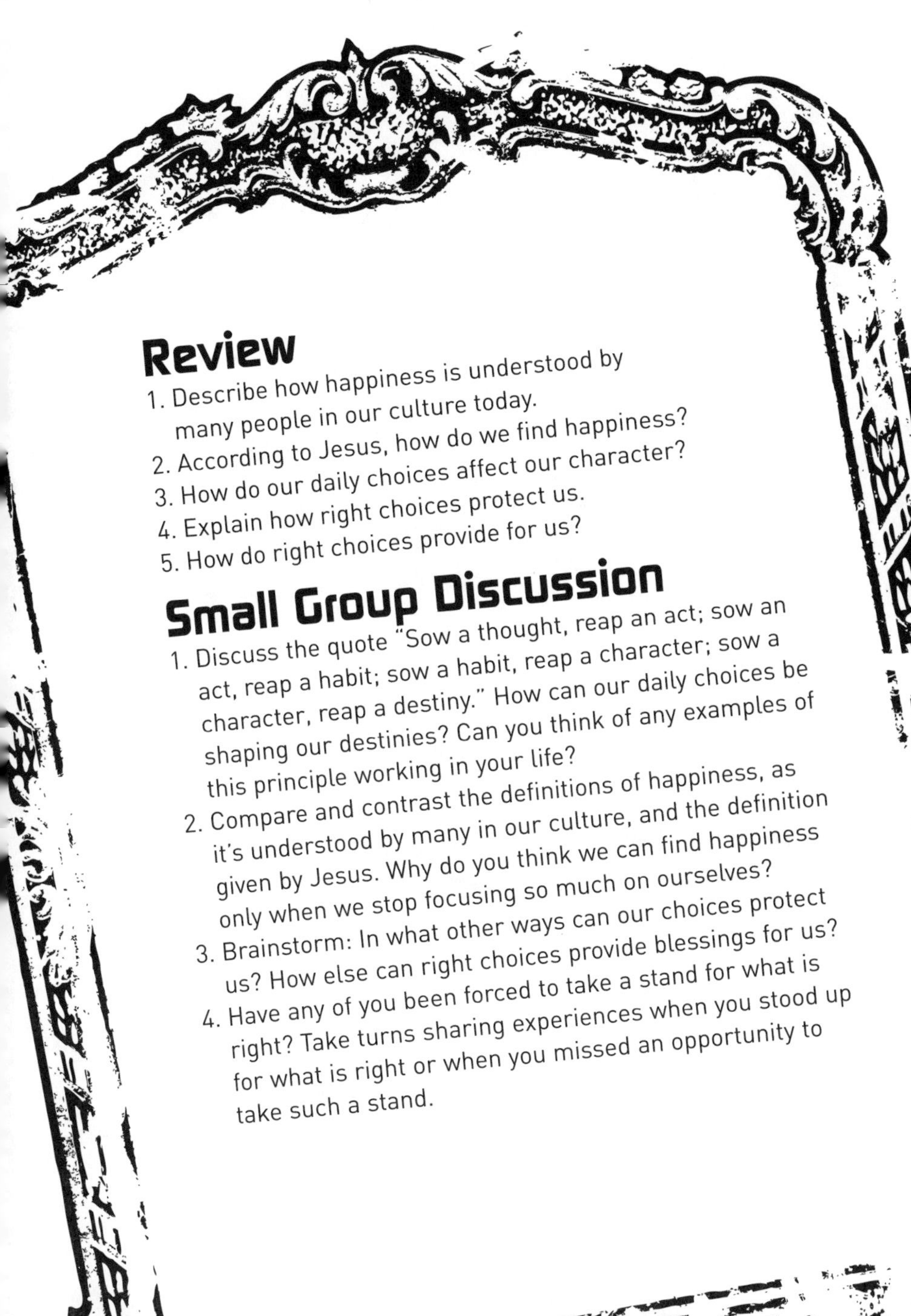

Review

1. Describe how happiness is understood by many people in our culture today.
2. According to Jesus, how do we find happiness?
3. How do our daily choices affect our character?
4. Explain how right choices protect us.
5. How do right choices provide for us?

Small Group Discussion

1. Discuss the quote "Sow a thought, reap an act; sow an act, reap a habit; sow a habit, reap a character; sow a character, reap a destiny." How can our daily choices be shaping our destinies? Can you think of any examples of this principle working in your life?
2. Compare and contrast the definitions of happiness, as it's understood by many in our culture, and the definition given by Jesus. Why do you think we can find happiness only when we stop focusing so much on ourselves?
3. Brainstorm: In what other ways can our choices protect us? How else can right choices provide blessings for us?
4. Have any of you been forced to take a stand for what is right? Take turns sharing experiences when you stood up for what is right or when you missed an opportunity to take such a stand.

How Can I Take a Stand for What is Right?

PURPOSE

To examine five of God's most important solutions that empower us to take a stand for what is right

In this chapter you will learn

- That God expects us to stand up for what is right even in today's immoral culture
- How God empowers us to live rightly through prayer and by his Holy Spirit
- The importance of reading God's Word and having quality Christian friends for making right choices
- Why it is so important to limit time watching and listening to secular entertainment

In 1958, high school students were interviewed and asked to list the main problems facing students. The answers were as follows:

- **Not doing homework**
- **Not respecting property—for example, throwing books**
- **Leaving lights on and doors and windows open**
- **Throwing spitballs in class**
- **Running through the halls**

When I show these responses to students they often respond with amazement and laughter. If you were asked to list the top problems facing youth today, what would you say? Recently I have been asking this question to hundreds of youth throughout the country. Not surprisingly, the results have been radically different. Here is what youth typically describe as the greatest problems facing young people today:

1. **Pressure to be involved sexually**
2. **Drugs and alcohol**
3. **Stress**
4. **Divorce and/or uninvolved parents**
5. **Struggles with self-image and fitting in**

Throughout the country, whenever I ask kids this question, I inevitably get the same results. So many young people feel overwhelmed, stressed, and pressured by a hostile culture. As you very well know, *the culture you are growing up in is radically different than the culture of your parents*. Some of the challenges you face have never been faced by any generation in history.

Faithfulness in marriage and purity before marriage are no longer the norm, but the exception. In fact, a recent *Newsweek* report indicated that marital infidelity is not only common, but expected. One million teens get pregnant each year. Thirty-three thousand Americans get an STD each day. Approximately one million abortions occur annually. Depression and stress are rampant. Fatherlessness and divorce are off the charts. Internet pornography use and sexual activity are at an all-time high. What are you to do?

You may feel so overwhelmed with school, sports, youth group, friends, and so many other responsibilities that you hardly have time to slow down and focus on God. Bombarded by music, movies, and other messages of promiscuity and compromise, who can honestly expect you to make right choices today? The answer to that question is simple: God does. God expects you to make moral choices. God's standards never change—even if ours do. And God not only expects us to stand up for what is right, he empowers us with the strength to do so.

GOD'S SOLUTION

I. God Empowers Us through His Holy Spirit

The hike I took with my friends during my junior year in college will be forever etched into my memory. Since I was the resident assistant for my college dorm, I decided to bring eighteen of my floormates up to the mountains of San Diego. This would be a weekend retreat of bonding and fun. For a good challenge we decided to take the three-mile hike to the top of Stonewall Mountain. While we were ready for the hike up the mountain, we were completely ill-prepared for the challenges of the journey down.

I had been living near the city lights of Los Angeles for only a couple of years, but I already had forgotten how dark a starry night can be in the mountains. And although we brought enough food, water, and other supplies for the trip to the top, we forgot to bring enough flashlights for a safe trek down. The sun set, dark clouds moved in, and we suddenly realized the urgency of getting home safely and quickly. By the time we gathered all our goods and set out for the trail, the night had become pitch black. And, when we retrieved the two flashlights that we did bring, we found out that *neither* of them worked!

Imagine nineteen college men trying to climb down a dark, windy mountainside without the necessary light to see what lay ahead. We began to feel somewhat panicked, but we realized that if we were going to make it down safely, we would have to work together. In fact, since some of the path could be dangerous, all nineteen of us held hands and inched our way down the mountain. Without the power of the flashlight, we were left to wander aimlessly through the darkness of the mountain. If we'd had good batteries, our trip would have been much less frustrating and dangerous. In fact, it would have been easy!

Just as a flashlight needs a power source to function properly, humans also need a power source. The Bible explains that the Holy Spirit is our true power source. Without the Holy Spirit we are left hopelessly alone to endure suffering and frustration. Yet when we accept Jesus Christ into our lives, God's power source automatically comes to live inside us. It is God who provides us with the strength to live rightly—a strength that we could not have on our own.

The Holy Spirit convicts us of sin and equips us with the ability to do what is right (see John 16:8, 13). The apostle Paul tells us, "No temptation has overtaken you but such as is common to man; and God is faithful, who will not allow you to be tempted beyond what you are able, but with temptation will provide the way of escape also, that you may be able to endure it" (1 Cor. 10:13). Although it sometimes seems impossible, God always equips us with a way out from temptation and addiction. Many members of Alcoholics Anonymous can testify to how the empowering love of God transformed them during the lowest point of their lives. Admitting our powerlessness, and asking God for help, is the first step in the process. Even in our biggest struggles in life—our addictions—God offers the power to free us.

Not only does God want us to avoid sin, he wants us to live significant and satisfying lives filled with love, joy, peace, patience, kindness, goodness, faithfulness, gentleness, and self-control (Gal. 5:22–23). But no matter how hard we try to do what is right, if we don't have God's power source—the Holy Spirit—we will be no more successful than trying to use a flashlight without a battery. The Holy Spirit is what gives us the strength to take a stand for what is right.

2. God Guides Us through Prayer

But having the power source inside us is not enough. There must also be a proper *connection* to the source. Let me explain. The summer after my college graduation was by far the hottest summer I have ever experienced. I was traveling with my dad and his team to various youth camps across the country. Unfortunately, we had to travel from southern Texas over to Tennessee and then back down to Florida—all in an RV without air conditioning! Well, we actually had AC for the first leg of the trip; but somehow it malfunctioned, and we had to endure heat well above 100° Fahrenheit (not to mention the unbelievable humidity) for the final two weeks of the trip. I can honestly remember sitting on the couch dripping with sweat as we traveled through the tip of Texas.

The distraction of the heat made it impossible for me to focus on my work. So I fanned myself with a book and watched the time pass by. Since none of us could figure out how to fix the problem, we decided to call a professional mechanic. In fact, we called about three or four mechanics throughout our trip, yet *none* of them could fix our problem either. Oh well, we figured, we'll just have to endure the heat.

We finally arrived at home, and decided to clean out the RV, to leave it clean for the owner from whom we borrowed it. I searched the back cupboard for remaining trash, and I will never forget what I found—a large circuit breaker that was the direct link to the power source of the bus. I looked more closely, and I realized that one of the circuits was disconnected—and guess which one it was!

The only broken circuit was the one linked directly to the AC. So I connected the circuit and instantly we had AC for fifteen minutes while we finished cleaning the RV. Throughout our journey we had endured so much hassle, frustration, and suffering simply because we were *disconnected* from the true power source. Throughout the entire trip we had the proper power; but with a broken circuit that we didn't know how to fix, we were unable to benefit from it.

While the Holy Spirit is our power source, prayer is our connection to that source. Without prayer we cannot utilize the power God has put within us. It's amazing how many young people are wandering around with the power of the Holy Spirit inside them—yet they're accomplishing very little. They get distracted by the cares of the world because they are disconnected from God's power source. Prayer is the circuit that connects us to God's incredible power.

I wish I could tell you that I understand how prayer works. But I can't. It is simply incomprehensible to me how an all-loving, all-powerful, all-knowing God can listen to, and act on, human prayers. Yet he does. It is simply beyond human ability to grasp how God can order his world in accordance with human desires. Yet this is exactly what God does every day.

God may not answer all our requests in the way we would like. And, realize it or not, this is a very good thing. This is a lesson Jim Carey's character Bruce, in the movie *Bruce Almighty*, finds out the hard way. God (played by Morgan Freeman) gives his powers to Bruce for a little while, to see whether he can handle them better. Desiring to please everyone, Bruce decides to answer all prayers with a resounding "Yes." What he fails to realize is that a positive answer for one person sometimes has a negative effect on that specific person, or on another. Surrounded by chaos, Bruce finally realizes that the real God is far more suited to run the world than he is. This is a lesson we can learn as well. God is in control. He hears our prayers, and he ultimately "causes all things to work together for good to those who love God, to those who are called according to His purpose" (Rom. 8:28).

3. God Speaks through His Word

Not too long ago I purchased a new Dell laptop with all the bells and whistles. To figure out the intricacies of my computer, do you think I pulled out my old Nintendo manual? Of course not! While my original Nintendo game system is very cool, it simply wouldn't help me figure out how to work my new Dell. The best way to figure out how to use my new computer is to ask the designer who has revealed his purpose in the instruction manual. In much the same way, God has revealed his purposes through the Bible. If we want to know the purpose of relationships, sex, or anything else in life, shouldn't we consult the ultimate Designer?

If we truly desire to be people of wisdom in a world in turmoil, we must spend time daily reading and studying the Bible, God's instruction manual for our lives. In order to know how God wants us to live, and before we even face moral challenges, we must learn God's standards. If we are unfamiliar with God's principles, we are more likely to make wrong choices that often carry heavy consequences. We must heed the advice God gave to Joshua over three thousand years ago: "This book of the law shall not depart from your mouth, but you shall meditate on it day and night, so that you may be careful to do according to all that is written in it; for then you will make your way prosperous, and then you will have success" (Josh. 1:8).

The Bible is the most unique and amazing book ever written. It deals with issues such as murder, rape, homosexuality, and many other controversial subjects. It was written by forty authors from all walks of life over a period of more than fifteen hundred years, yet it has one message about God's redemption of mankind. It has sold more copies, been translated into more languages, and has had a greater impact on the history of the world *than any other book—ever*. While it may take some time and discipline to understand the Bible (especially challenging books such as Leviticus and Revelation), it is well worth the effort. If you desire to better understand the Bible, you might consider some of the Bible study books offered in the student series also published by Broadman & Holman.

4. God Desires That We Hang Out with Christian Friends

David has always been my favorite character in the Bible. It always amazed me how David, a mere shepherd-boy, could single-handedly defeat the great and mighty Goliath. During his lifetime, David reigned over the world's most powerful kingdom. And of all the people who have ever lived, David is the only one God called "a man after my own heart." Yet despite his godly qualities, David made some costly mistakes for which he paid a heavy price.

Rather than going to war to support his troops like a

king was supposed to do, David stayed home in Jerusalem one year. And one night, while he was walking around on the roof, he saw a beautiful woman—named Bathsheba—bathing below. This was a critical moment for David—would he choose to look away and do the right thing, or would he indulge in his sinful desires? David not only chose to indulge, but he had his servants go get her so he could sleep with her. Shortly thereafter David received word saying that Bathsheba was pregnant. Desperately trying to cover up his sin, David lied and ultimately had Uriah, Bathsheba's husband, murdered.

I have often wondered where David's friends were when he made this decision. Did he have friends around him to encourage him to do the right thing, or did he think he could stand up for what is right alone? Could David have avoided such pain in his life if he had better friends around him? This same question applies to you: *what type of friends do you hang out with*? Do you spend time with people who will encourage you to be the type of person God wants you to be, or do you spend time with people who will bring you down? While there may be nothing wrong with hanging out with non-Christians, we *all* need the support of close, Christian friends. Truthfully speaking, there are few people in life that will have a greater impact on your choices than the friends you hang out with. This is why Paul warns us, "Do not be deceived: 'Bad company corrupts good morals'" (1 Cor. 15:33). In the same book Paul says, "I wrote you in my letter not to associate with immoral people" (1 Cor. 5:9).

Good friends not only keep us from trouble, they help us live wise and courageous lives. Proverbs 27:17 says, "Iron sharpens iron, so one man sharpens another." Great friendships, rooted in biblical truth, help us become the type of people God wants us to be. This is why J. R. R. Tolkien considered Sam to be the essential character of his trilogy *The Lord of the Rings*. Tolkien realized that those who accomplish great things in life have the strength of a faithful companion. Frodo could never have accomplished his task without the enduring friendship of Sam. Similarly, we will be at a great disadvantage to take a stand for what is right without devoted friends who hold us accountable for our decisions.

Members of Alcoholics Anonymous understand the power of friendship and accountability. They are a community of wounded people who, despite their common addiction, choose not to drink. They have each other. They share phone numbers. They have sponsors. And they have prayer. But without the support of the community, they could not succeed. They mutually strengthen each other for the difficult challenge of remaining sober, an impossible task alone. No matter how strong we think we are, none of us can survive alone—period.

5. Limit Intake of Secular Entertainment

Few people understand how much their music and movies have an impact on their choices. In fact, most people think they are immune from media influences. But all studies indicate the exact opposite: *movies and music deeply influence the way people think about the world and how they act*.

Recently white supremacy has been making a significant comeback among youth. How do you think they attract new recruits? According to Byron Calvert, producer of a "white power" record company, the way to persuade students is through the use of music. "We hook 'em with the music," he says. "The kids go right for the music, and the lyrics, at first, are almost secondary. It's a very insidious way of indoctrinating kids into a whole lifestyle."[1] In other words, music producers prey on young people, like you, through music.

While all media messages may not be as forthcoming as white supremacy, you are still bombarded daily by hundreds of lies, especially in the area of sex. It's only a matter of time before some of these lies start to influence the way you think and act. Let me explain. Did you know that one in three sexually active teenagers has a sexually transmitted disease (STD)? Yet, in all the casual sex portrayed in the media, how many times can you remember a character contracting a STD? It would be unusual if you could even think of one occurrence. *The point is simple: while many people suffer emotional and physical trauma in real life, rarely does anyone on TV pay any consequences.* The lack of connection between actions and consequences on television affects the way most people view sex in real life.

My students often tell me that television and music don't affect their behavior very much. Yet, there is a simple question I like to ask: If there is no relationship between television commercials and viewers' behavior, why do American businesses spend billions of dollars each year on advertising—for prime time television alone? Advertisers understand a simple truth: what we watch with our eyes and listen to with our ears affects our decisions. This is why Proverbs 4:25 warns, "Let your eyes look directly ahead, and let your gaze be fixed straight in front of you." In other words, don't compromise your values by listening to music or watching movies that will influence your decision making away from God's desires.

CONCLUSION

How can I be a moral person in such an immoral society? The answer is simple. You can't! Trying to live a moral life on your own is like trying to use a flashlight without the batteries or using air conditioning with a broken circuit. It simply can't be done. But God offers us another way: being empowered with the Holy Spirit through prayer, studying God's Word and applying it to our lives, surrounding ourselves with other believers, and limiting our intake of secular media. By utilizing these tools in our lives, we will be able to be moral people in an immoral society.

Review

1. How does God empower us through his Holy Spirit?
2. What role should prayer play in our lives?
3. Why is the Bible important for living a moral life? What makes the Bible unique?
4. Why is it so important that we spend time with other believers?
5. Why should we limit how much time we spend watching/listening to secular media?

Small Group Discussion

1. What would you say are the greatest problems facing your generation today? Do you agree with the assessment of the students interviewed from around the country at the beginning of the chapter?
2. If you were Satan, what things would you do to prevent youth today from living morally?
3. How much do music and movies affect the way youth think and act? Is it possible to listen to music that glorifies sexuality and rebellion without being personally influenced?this principle working in your life?
2. Compare and contrast the definitions of happiness, as it's understood by many in our culture, and the definition given by Jesus. Why do you think we can find happiness only when we stop focusing so much on ourselves?
3. Brainstorm: In what other ways can our choices protect us? How else can right choices provide blessings for us?
4. Have any of you been forced to take a stand for what is right? Take turns sharing experiences when you stood up for what is right or when you missed an opportunity to take such a stand.

Is There Such a Thing as Truth

PURPOSE

To understand the nature and importance of truth, as well as learn how to defend truth against popular objections

In this chapter you will learn

- Why truth is so important for a successful and meaningful life
- How to understand and define truth
- The difference between subjective and objective truth and why this distinction is so crucial for our decision making
- How to defend the reality of truth against popular objections
- That truth was personally embodied in the person of Jesus Christ

Down through the ages, people have asked the same question Pilate asked Jesus two thousand years ago: **Is there such a thing as truth?** And if truth is real, how can we know it? How can we be sure moral truths even exist?

One little girl's story demonstrates how many young people today would determine the answers to these questions. For an elementary "show-and-tell" this young girl brought in a puppy for the class to enjoy. The classmates began to wonder about the gender of the puppy, but none of them knew how to ascertain it. The young girl raised her hand, "I know how we can tell," she explained. "We can vote."[1] While we may snicker at her childish response, she illustrated the most common view of truth in our culture—majority rules. When absolutes are taken out of the picture, people are free to create their own version of truth.

What this perspective fails to consider is that truth, as my seminary professor J. P. Moreland observed, is "disgustingly indifferent" to what we decide. We can no more decide on truth than I can decide to have a million dollars in my wallet! If we could merely decide truth, then I decide to be the greatest basketball player in the world. You could just decide to have all A's on your report card (wouldn't that be great!). But obviously we cannot merely decide on truth, because truth is indifferent to what we think and believe. We can choose our beliefs, but we can't choose the truth. Hopefully our beliefs will match up with reality, but we have no power to create truth any more than we can decide the gender of a puppy by voting on it.

WHY IS TRUTH IMPORTANT?

Dr. Francis Beckwith, philosophy professor at Baylor University, had a very skeptical student in his ethics class who questioned everything he said. She was always challenging his conclusions. One day she said, with an air of smugness, "Dr. Beckwith, why is truth important?" After thinking for a moment, he gave this witty reply: "Well, would you like the *true* answer or the *false* one?" This question silenced her because she realized a profound point—that her very question assumed that there was such a thing as truth. Deep-rooted in the hearts of young men and women is the awareness that truth is a necessary bedrock for life. In fact, we cannot even live without truth. There are three more reasons why truth is so important:

1. Without truth we live in a world of tragedy. Many of you are familiar with the tragic story of the Donner Party. In 1846, this group of eighty-seven people headed west in hopes of building a new future. They took a "shortcut" to save time, but on the map was *false* information. Caught in a vicious snowstorm for months, this group of people was forced to cannibalism to survive. Forty-one of the people died in one of the most horrific tales in American history. Why was there so much tragedy? Simply because they were not given *true* information about their journey. We are also on a journey where we have the choice of following truth or experiencing tragedy. More feelings have been hurt, lives have been lost, and damage has been done because people sidestep the truth. The apostle Paul tells us that people perish because they avoid the truth (2 Thess. 2:8–10).

2. Truth is a compass for our lives. F-14 fighter pilots often experience a phenomenon known as vertigo. When this happens a pilot can become disoriented as to how fast and high he is going. If he relies on his emotions, sensations, or memory he may lose control of the flight and crash. But there is one thing that will *never* lie to the pilot—his instruments. His instruments will help him determine his height and speed so he can safely control the plane. Similarly, we need a standard in our decision making. This standard is truth. Truth, like a compass, helps us make wise and informed decisions.

3. Truth has consequences. The Christian faith, as well as its rivals, essentially contains claims about the world, which are either true or false. In addition, competing worldview truth claims often have very different consequences for life. As C. S. Lewis put it, "We are now getting to the point at which different beliefs about the universe lead to different behavior. Religion involves a series of statements about facts, which must be either true of false. If they are true, one set of conclusions will follow about the right sailing of the human fleet; if they are false, quite a different set."[2] Your view of relationships, sex, money, and the future all depends on your view of truth.

WHAT IS TRUTH?

While people often talk about truth, few can define what it is. Yet if we are unable to define what truth is, how will we know when we have it? How will we know we are not being deceived?

The classical definition of truth, which was held by virtually everyone until the nineteenth century, is known as the *correspondence theory of truth,* which is roughly the idea that truth is a matter of a proposition (belief, thought, statement) corresponding to reality; something is true when reality is the way a statement represents it to be.[3] In other words, a statement is true if it matches up with the way the world actually is. Truth is simply "telling it like it is."

For example, if I make the claim that there is a red Hummer 2 in my driveway, this statement is either true or false (it is impossible that the H2 is *both* there and *not* there at the same time!). If there in fact is a red H2 in my driveway, then my statement is true. If there is no red H2, then, to my chagrin, my statement is false. A statement is simply true when it matches up with reality. The Bible assumes this commonsense view of truth. Here are three random examples from the Scriptures:

- Pharaoh wanted to know the facts as they corresponded to his real dream (Gen. 41).
- The ninth commandment of the Bible warns against false testimony, which is testimony that does not correspond to the facts (Exod. 20:16).
- Jesus gave Judas the facts as they corresponded to the real world, namely that Judas would be the one who would betray him (Matt. 26:23–25).

This view of truth, as you can see, is the standard way we use truth every day. We know things are true when they match up with the real world; and we know they are false when they do not match up with the real world. But what most young Christians don't realize is that many people change this definition of truth when they begin to talk about morality. They smuggle in a different definition of truth and catch many young people unaware. To avoid this snare, it is critical to understand the following two kinds of truth.

TWO KINDS OF TRUTH

Subjective Truths

Knowing truth helps us to make right moral decisions. But not all decisions in life deal with morality. Most choices we make, in fact, are not moral choices at all. Should we go bowling tonight, or should we go to the movies? Do I prefer Chocolate-Peanut-Butter-Cup or Cookies-and-Cream ice cream? Should I wear my green shirt or my black shirt? These are personal choices relative to the individual. The way one would answer these questions would be considered *subjective* truths. The phrase "Chocolate ice cream is the best flavor" may be true for you but not for me. These types of truths are based on preference or feeling and can easily change.[4]

Objective Truths

But moral choices are not subjective, like choosing an ice cream flavor. Rather, moral choices are more like insulin.[5] Insulin, as many of you know, controls diabetes. It doesn't matter if I think chocolate ice cream will control diabetes because the truth is that it will not. Controlling diabetes correctly requires insulin. Regardless of my personal preference or feelings, the statement "Insulin controls diabetes" is an *objective* truth.

Objective truths, as opposed to subjective preferences, are based on the external world. They are related to the world independently of how we think or feel. For example, the sentences "1 + 2 = 3," "George Washington was the first president of the United States," and "Sacramento is the capital of California" are all objective truths.

Similarly, moral choices are choices between what is objectively right and what is objectively wrong. That's why we feel guilty when we make wrong moral choices as opposed to wrong non-moral choices. We might feel *regret* when we realize our green shirt may have looked better than our black one, but regret is different than guilt.

Just imagine for a moment what would happen if morality was subjective (i.e., a matter of personal taste) rather than objective. If this were true, then how could we condemn rape or murder, for wouldn't they be the result of personal preference, like choosing an ice cream flavor? If morality was subjective then there would be no real difference between a father who nurtures and cares for his children and a father who molests his children. Each father made a personal choice, and that choice was "true" for him.

The Personal Side of Truth

There is a sense in which moral choices are personal, because we each have to make them, and we are each personally accountable for our actions. But they are *more* than personal because their intrinsic rightness or wrongness does not depend on our individual choice. Moral choices are personal in the same way as when you take a science test: *you* take the test and *you* are given an individual grade. There is a right answer to each question on the science test—you may get it right, or you may get it wrong. But your mere choosing does not make your answer right; the correct answer exists independently of your choosing it.

Of course, making real-life moral choices is different than making choices on a test. In the classroom you have a test booklet in front of you; but in real life moral dilemmas, there is a world in front of you. There are right moral choices, and there are wrong moral choices. Morality is about the real, objective world. This is why the question of the morality of abortion is not a question of preference—like choosing an ice cream flavor. Rather, it is an objective question about the real world. Homosexuality is not merely a question of sexual preference; it is a question about what is right to do sexually and what is wrong (we will discuss this in detail in chap. 8).

ABSOLUTE TRUTH

When my brother-in-law turned fourteen, he shot up in height. It seemed like every couple of weeks he was passing up someone in the family. And it was not long before he was anxious to demonstrate that he was taller than I. Of course, since I was the older "brother," I had to do everything I could not to let this happen. Since it was difficult to judge by the naked eye, we needed an outside standard. So we took off our shoes and used an official scale. To my chagrin, he had just barely passed me up! Now he's six feet five inches and taller than anyone in the whole family!

Without the final standard we never would have solved our dilemma on that day. We needed a standard to determine the truth. If we stop and reflect for a moment we realize that our entire existence relies on standards. We have standards to measure the size of shoes, the distance to another city, the temperature of water, and the score in a sports competition. Without standards our world would be in chaos. Standards are so important that we could not function without them. Just imagine for a moment what life would be like if we had no standards.

- How would you know what kind of gas to put in your car?
- How would you know what size pants to buy?
- How would you know how much a new video game costs?
- How would you know, without the measure of time, when the school day ended?

A society without standards is a society in disarray. If people could drive on whatever side of the road they desired or as fast as they wanted, society would be out of control. If there were no standard of measurement for commerce, honest business would be nearly impossible. In order for society to thrive, there must be common standards of measurement and conduct. While the standards set by our government (such as the price of gas, traffic laws, and certain monetary policies) have an impact on society, they are merely *conditional* standards. If the authorities behind these standards decided to change them, they could do so.

But we seldom reflect enough to realize that our conditional standards point to a higher standard beyond our control—an *absolute* standard. For example, we have decided to measure time through the use of seconds, minutes, hours, days, years, and so on. However, beyond our measurements is a standard outside of our control. For example, can we control the length of a day or can we control the rotation of the earth and its orbit around the sun? Of course not! We cannot control these factors because they are beyond human control—they are part of a standard outside human jurisdiction.

Similarly, we can measure length through inches, feet, and miles. But can we change the distance from the earth to the moon or from the sun to the outer edges of the universe? We can use man-made measurements to determine length, but we have to admit that there are distances beyond our grasp. The standards of distance, as well as many other standards, point us to a higher standard—an absolute standard—beyond our control.

BEYOND US

Like the standards just mentioned, absolute truth is also beyond human control. My parents used to give me a curfew to be home by 11:00 p.m., but that was merely for me in my family—not an absolute truth. Absolute truth, on the other hand, is *truth that is true for all people, for all times, and for all places*. It is objective, universal, and constant. Absolute truth is real and solid, whether we choose to believe in it or not, just as the moon is real even when we cannot see it on a cloudy night.

Absolute truth is true—whether or not anyone believes it.
Absolute truth is true—whether or not anyone follows it.
Absolute truth is true—whether or not it is discovered.
Absolute truth is true—whether or not it "works" in the way we want it to.
Absolute truth is true—whether or not we agree with it.

An Absolute Moral Standard

The standards that we have seen point us to a greater standard, one beyond human control—absolute truth. This same intuition that drives us to make standards in the physical world also exists in the moral world. Everyone knows naturally that certain things are morally wrong. It is common sense that there are moral absolutes beyond us. Even people who claim not to believe in God know that certain things are right and certain things are wrong.

Ask this question to anyone: If twenty male youths decide to rape a handicapped girl, would it be OK? Would the number of people involved make it right? If society said it was OK, would that make it acceptable? Of course not! Everyone knows deep down in their hearts that this is wrong. We know this is wrong not because of what our culture or society may say but because of the nature of rape.

We know that torturing babies for amusement is wrong. We know that honesty is right. We know that terrorism is wrong. We know that unselfishness is right. We know that stealing is wrong. We know that courage is right. How do we really know such things? In Romans 2:12–15, Paul tells us that God placed the moral law on our hearts. People know morality is real because they are moral beings. C. S. Lewis put it this way: "Whenever you find a man who says he does not believe in a real Right and Wrong, you will find the same man going back on this a moment later. He may break his promise to you, but if you try breaking one to him he will be complaining, 'It's not fair' before you can say Jack Robinson. It seems, then, we are forced to believe in a real Right and Wrong. People may sometimes be mistaken about them, just as people sometimes get their sums wrong; but they are not a matter of mere taste and opinion any more than the multiplication table."[6]

Just as God is the source of the physical rules of the universe, he is also the source of its moral rules. As the law of gravity is inherent in the nature of matter, so is the law of love inherent in the nature of man. Philosopher Peter Kreeft put it this way: "The law of gravity is true because that's the *nature* of matter. The law of love is true because that's the *nature* of man: man was *designed* to love, as matter was designed to attract."[7]

This has a powerfully practical application for the task of defending moral truths. Christians need not appeal *solely* to the Bible as the basis for criticizing public sins such as abortion or pornography. While these are sins against God, they are also sins against the nature of man, against natural law. Therefore, we can call on all people of good will (regardless of their religious persuasion) to defend the rights of the unborn and to protect the sanctity of marriage. We do not want to be seen as "imposing our religious values" on everyone, but rather as arguing persuasively and lovingly for common moral truths.

THE PERSON OF TRUTH

When Pilate, nearly twenty centuries ago, questioned Jesus about truth, he failed to realize something profound: Truth was standing right in his presence. Jesus said, "I am the way, and the truth, and the life" (John 14:6). Pilate was not just discussing truth in his Jerusalem palace that day; he was literally looking at it with his own two eyes. Truth was standing before him, clothed in human flesh! Jesus Christ, "who came from the Father, full of grace and truth," is the very embodiment and essence of absolute moral and spiritual truth itself (John 1:14 NIV).

Truth is much more than a mere abstract fact or concept: it is inescapably *relational.* Truth can be found in the person of Jesus of Nazareth. As you will see in the next chapter, it is the very person and nature of God that defines truth. It is not something he measures up to. It is not something he declares. It is not an arbitrary decision he makes. It is something he *is* in the core of his being.

We cannot separate the idea of truth from the person of truth—Jesus Christ. This is why Jesus told Peter, "Follow Me!" (John 21:19). Rather than telling Peter merely to follow certain rules, obey certain commands, or live out certain teachings, Jesus' final instruction to Peter was: "Follow Me!" Jesus knew that Peter could only fully understand what it meant to know truth if he was first willing to follow Jesus with all his heart. Unless we understand and live the truth within the context of a personal relationship with God, it will ultimately lead to legalism. Scriptural commands and rules should no longer be seen as merely instructions to obey but rather as ways to deepen a relationship with a living person. If we want to seek truth, we ought to seek Jesus, for Jesus is the very embodiment of truth.

Understanding Jesus Christ as the absolute embodiment of truth means that:

- **Objective truth cannot be subjectively created;** truth is and comes from the objective, absolute person of Christ. As John wrote: "For the Law was given through Moses; grace and truth were realized through Jesus Christ" (John 1:17).
- **Objective truth cannot be relative** and change from person to person, from community to community, because Jesus is the incarnation of the God who "never changes or casts shifting shadows" (James 1:17 NLT). As the book of Hebrews says, "Jesus Christ is the same yesterday, today, and forever" (13:8 HCSB).
- **All truth cannot be equal,** because Jesus didn't claim to be "a" truth, one that is equal to all others. His claim was exclusive; he claimed to be the one and only truth, the only way to God. "I am the way, and the truth, and the life; no one comes to the

Father but through Me" (John 14:6). These are not the words of someone who is "one among many," someone who is "equal" to all others; those are the words of one who has no equal.

RESPONDING TO OBJECTIONS

"There is no truth." The problem with this phrase is that it is *self-contradictory*. In other words, the sentence refutes itself through its very existence. Let me explain. At the commencement of his letter to Titus, Paul gives some advice to Titus, who is ministering to the Cretan people. Titus is being confronted with some hostile ideas. Paul quotes Epimenides, a Cretan. Paul tells Titus: "One of themselves, a prophet of their own, said, 'Cretans are always liars, evil beasts, lazy gluttons'" (Titus 1:12). Any astute Bible reader would catch the irony in this statement. If *all* Cretans are liars, then can how Epimenides himself really be trusted?[8] It would be like me, as a Californian, saying, "You can't trust anybody from California."

The statements "Cretans are always liars" and "there is no truth" suffer from the same defect: *both statements contradict themselves*. The statement "there is no truth" is a truth claim about at least one thing—namely, that "there is no truth." Yet this statement contradicts itself by claiming that truth does not exist. Here are some other examples of self-contradictory statements:

- There are no English sentences with more than five words. (You just read one!)
- There is no such thing as absolute truth. (Is that absolutely true?)
- We cannot be sure about anything. (Are you sure about that?)
- Never say the word "never." (Too late, you already said it!)

All four of these statements—like the phrase "there is no truth"—contain the seeds of their own refutation. They undermine themselves by contradicting their own standard for truth. There is no way to escape the fact that truth exists.

"But moral truths cannot be tested by science." It is true that morality cannot be detected by the scientific method. But so what? There are many truths—such as historical truths, relational truths, or truths of self-awareness—that also cannot be tested by science. For example, the fact that George Washington was the first president

WE DON'T CREATE TRUTH, WE DISCOVER IT.

of the United States cannot be ascertained through scientific investigation, but we are fully justified in claiming to know this fact. While moral truths also do not appear to the physical senses, they appear to our inner sense—conscience. While we cannot prove scientifically that it is wrong to torture babies for fun or that love is better than hate, we are still justified in claiming that we know them to be true.

"It may be true for you, but not for me."

Although this is a commonly used phrase, we must ask, can truth exist solely for the person who believes it? Can something be true for one person but not another? Beneath this phrase lies a deep-seated confusion between the concepts of *truth* and *belief*. Clearly, we each are entitled to our own beliefs (at least in America, the land of the free), but does this mean that we each have our own respective truths? Objective truth, as we discussed earlier, is independent of our beliefs. But beliefs, on the other hand, are necessarily personal. Therefore, when we consider the nature of truth it makes no sense to say that something is true for you but not for me. A brief illustration will be helpful.

Imagine that you and your friend encounter a green apple lying on a table. Your friend believes the inside is rotten and full of worms. But you, on the other hand, believe it is crisp and worm-free. Can your varying beliefs about the apple create two distinct truths that each of you experience as reality? The only way to solve the dilemma is to slice open the apple and observe its inside. Then you will be in a position to discover the truth about the apple—if it has worms or not. The instant the apple is sliced, the truth will be revealed and the false beliefs will be exposed. The truth about the apple exists independently of you and your friend's beliefs about it.[9]

"I can create my own truth." We do create rules such as driving on the right side of the road. Society could just as easily have created a different rule to drive on the left. But we do not invent truth, and we do not invent morality, any more than we invent the length of a day. We cannot make lying right, and we cannot make murder good. We are not free to create our own values, and we are not free to create our own truths. We are free to accept or reject truth, just as we are free to obey or disobey moral laws. Similarly, we do not invent the law of gravity, but we are free to disregard it, to jump off a building and believe we can fly. But our mere disregard for the truth does nothing to change truth itself. We don't *create* truth, we *discover* it.

"Sincerity is more important than truth." "It doesn't matter *what* people believe," we often hear, "it's how sincerely they hold to those beliefs." People of all religions demonstrate the same degree of zeal as the best of Christians. So how can we, as Christians, criticize such commitment? Shouldn't sincerity count for something?

It is important to remember that sincerity is *necessary* for salvation but not *sufficient*. If the claim that "It doesn't matter what people believe, as long as they're sincere" were true, then the sincerity of the 9/11 terrorists or the Unabomber would be admirable. But we all know that their actions—despite their sincerity—were dead wrong. Even Jesus was crucified by religious leaders with the utmost sincerity. As integral as sincerity is for belief, it cannot be alienated from truth.

"Truth is what works." Many young people say, "If it works for you, then it's as true as it needs to be. No one has the right to judge you or question what you have chosen as true for yourself." While this is a popular view today, there are two significant problems. First, some truths don't "work." For example, the truth that there is no largest prime number has no practical use, but surely it is true. Second, sometimes falsehoods may actually "work" in our favor ("The dog ate my homework"). Although truth does work (as God intends it to), what "works" is not always true.

"Truth changes over time." One of the most common ways truth is attacked is the claim that it changes over time. What is true for people today was not true for people in the past. Obviously, if what is true now was not true in the past, then what is true now may cease to be true in the future. If we follow this line of reasoning, truth quickly loses its practical importance.

Inevitably, the example given to defend this view is the flat-earth vs. round-earth dilemma. I once had a girl say to me: "People used to believe that the earth was flat, but now they believe it is round. See, truth changes." What this girl fails to understand, as we have already noted, is the distinction between *belief* and *truth*. While people may once have believed that the earth was flat, common sense tells us that the earth has *always* been round, despite changing beliefs. While beliefs may vary, truth is constant.

CONCLUSION

Truth, as we have seen, is important for every aspect of our lives. Life without truth is a life of tragedy. But when we know truth we are equipped to make wise decisions and to flourish as human beings. While truth occurs when our beliefs match reality, truth is also much more than that. Two thousand years ago truth was embodied in the person of Jesus Christ. Scriptural commands and rules are not merely instructions to obey, but rather ways to deepen a relationship with Jesus Christ. And when we personally experience the truth of Jesus Christ, we will be empowered to live a bold and meaningful life.

Review

1. Give three reasons why truth is important.
2. Define truth and give an example of how this definition applies to the Bible.
3. Explain the difference between subjective and objective truth.
4. Are the following statements *objective truths* or *subjective truths*? How do you know?
   - The Los Angeles Lakers are the most fun team to watch in the NBA.
   - Diet soda has fewer calories than regular soda.
   - Sacramento is the capital of California.
   - Pink is prettier than red.
   - Abortion is wrong.
   - Jake Burnett plays for the Jackson City Boilers.
   - Brunettes are more attractive than blonds.
   - Homosexuality is immoral.
5. What is absolute truth? How do we know absolute truth is real?
6. How do we know that moral truths are real?
7. What did Pilate fail to realize when he questioned Jesus about the nature of truth? What implications does this truth have for us today?
8. Respond to the following objections:

   There is no truth.

   Moral truths cannot be tested by science.

   It may be true for you, but not for me.

   I can create my own truth.

   Sincerity is more important than truth.

   Truth is what works.

   Truth changes over time.

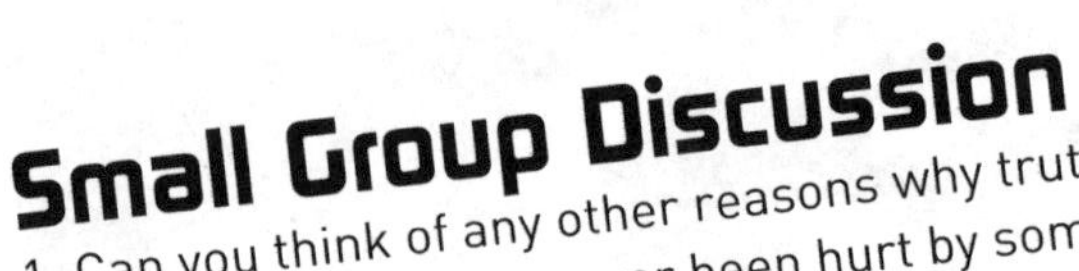

Small Group Discussion

1. Can you think of any other reasons why truth is important? Have you ever been hurt by someone who didn't tell the truth? Have you ever had to face consequences for ignoring truth?
2. What would the world look like if there were no standards of measurement? What would the world look like if there were no moral standard for right and wrong?
3. Is it better to face truth or deny it? Do you think most people accept or reject truth? Defend your answer.

Who Are You to Judge?

PURPOSE

To understand and evaluate moral relativism and see why the existence of God is the only adequate foundation for making moral judgments

In this chapter you will learn

- The difference between moral relativism and ethical absolutism
- How to recognize the three fatal flaws of relativism
- That the existence of God provides the only firm foundation for morals
- Five reasons why we can have confidence in God's existence
- That the Bible commands followers of Jesus to judge
- Strategies for how we should respond as Christians in the midst of our tolerant and non-judgmental culture

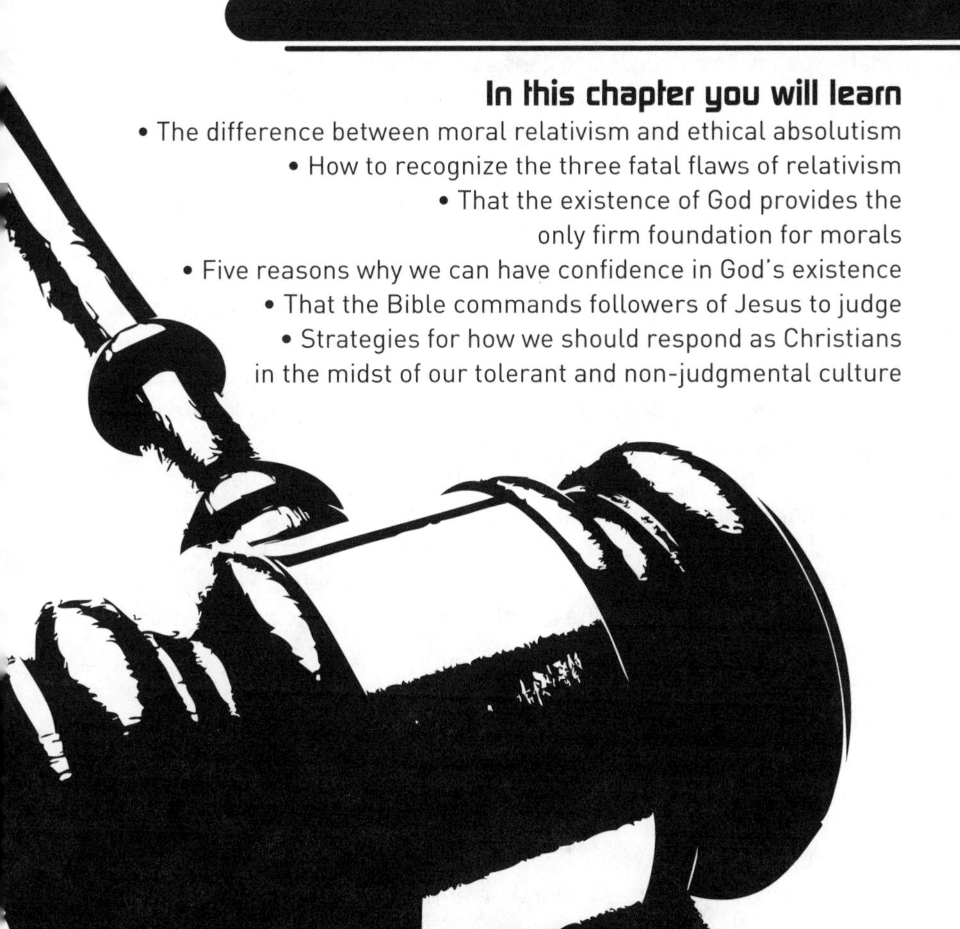

As the movie The *Matrix* begins, the human race is being deceived by a group of artificially intelligent robots. The robots are harvesting the bodies of the humans for battery power but are controlling their minds through a mental simulation known as the Matrix. Because their minds are being controlled by the robots, human beings are fooled into believing their perception of the world is real. In fact, they have no idea that their entire world is a lie. Yet one small renegade group of humans manages to escape the false reality of the Matrix and attempts to "free the minds" of the rest of the human race. Neo (played by Keanu Reaves) is given the option of escaping the Matrix by knowing the truth. He hesitates to confront reality because everything familiar to him tells him the Matrix is real. Yet there is a yearning inside Neo driving him toward truth. After Neo finally makes the decision to be freed, he looks back with amazement at the "world that had been pulled over his eyes."

In a similar way, there is a world that has been pulled over your eyes—the world of *moral relativism*. This worldview has shaped your entire generation, yet many of you don't even realize it. Let me explain.

Not long ago I was speaking at a youth rally on the topic of sexuality. In the middle of my talk a girl interrupted and echoed the five words I so often hear from young people today: "Who are you to judge?" In other words, she was saying that I had no right to make moral judgments because all views are equal. This girl, like the rest of your generation, has grown up in a culture of moral relativism that prides itself on accepting many truths. You have been taught to be tolerant of all beliefs, without judgment, without being critical, and to think that no one way is better than another. In fact, the moment you claim to have *the truth* you are labeled as arrogant, bigoted, and judgmental. The fact that I had the gall to make a moral judgment about sex was very upsetting to this young girl.

Because moral relativism is so ingrained in the media and the educational system, most of you don't even realize how much this false worldview has infiltrated your thinking. Professor Allen Bloom, author of *The Closing of the American Mind*, put it this way: "There is one thing a professor can be absolutely certain of: almost every student entering the university believes, or says he believes, that truth is relative. The students, of course, cannot defend their opinion. It is something with which they have been *indoctrinated*."[1]

Like the struggle in *The Matrix*, there is a fierce battle being waged in the world today. But this battle is not between robots and humans; it is between those who hold to moral relativism and those who believe in absolute truth. If you are willing to open your eyes and embrace reality, you will see that this is a battle waging for the very souls of your generation. Do you yearn for the truth?

TRUTH VS. RELATIVISM

Imagine a multiple-car collision at a central intersection near your school. Immediately after the accident all the parties run into the intersection sharing their side of the story. One says, "You cut me off!" Another says, "I have the right of way!" And a third cries, "Don't you know that a red light means STOP!?" Even pedestrians who saw the accident from the sidewalk put in their two cents about the facts. Then, perhaps, finally the perpetrator steps forward and confesses: "It was my fault. I reached to turn off my radio and lost control of the car."

Despite all the post-accident deliberations, one thing is clear: an accident happened. And in a matter of time, the truth will be known. We believe there is an objective truth about the accident. Eventually, a description of the accident will surface that corresponds to reality.[2] In the same way, we live our lives as if objective truth is real—if we can only discover it. When making decisions we consider facts and weigh evidence. We do our best to arrive at truth, and then we live accordingly. Enter the relativist. To the *relativist*, there are no truths that apply to all people, for all places, for all times. He argues that since everyone has a different viewpoint, the truth of the accident scene cannot be known. In fact, some would argue that we could not even be sure the accident happened in the first place!

Observing the world, the relativist comes to a simple conclusion: *there is too much disagreement about too many things for truth to be absolute*. Since people disagree so vehemently about issues such as ethics, politics, and religion, isn't it arrogant to claim that one perspective is correct and *all* the others are false? While there does seem to be an intuitive appeal to moral relativism, most people fail to realize the shocking implications that follow from accepting relativism as the basis for morality.

Most young people who make the claim that we shouldn't judge fail to fully grasp the scope of their denial. When we lose the ability to make moral judgments we can no longer make a distinction between the actions of Mother Theresa and Hitler. How can we say that torturing two-year-olds for fun is either right or wrong? How can we distinguish between good and evil? When young people give up the right to make moral judgments they give up more ground than they ever imagined. This became evident to me in a conversation that I had several years ago with my dad.

Some time ago, when I was a senior in high school, my parents took me to see Stephen Spielberg's movie *Schindler's List*.

As we left the theater we were surrounded by a sober crowd, many of whom were commenting on the atrocities inflicted upon the Jews by the Nazis. People were talking about how evil the Nazis were to treat humans with such indignity. My dad turned to me abruptly and said, "Sean, do you believe the Holocaust was wrong—morally wrong?"

I quickly answered, "Yes, of course."

My dad continued: "Almost everyone walking out of the theater would say the Holocaust was wrong. But what basis do they have for making that judgment? Could they answer *why* it was wrong? Can you answer why it was wrong?" Although I gave it my best shot, I was stumped. I knew the Bible said killing was wrong, but I didn't know *why*. I wondered, *Who am I to judge the actions of another culture from another time?*

As we headed to a restaurant, my dad began to share some lessons with me that I have never forgotten.

"Most people in America subscribe to a view of morality called 'cultural relativism,'" he said. "In other words, they believe that whatever is acceptable in that culture is moral; if the majority of people in a culture say a thing is 'right,' then it is right."

I took a bite out of my bacon cheeseburger, and my dad continued: "That's why many Americans will say that abortion is OK, because the majority of Americans—and Congress and the Supreme Court—have accepted it. If the majority thinks its OK, it must be OK, right?

"But there's a problem with that," he explained. "If that is true, then how can we say the murdering of six million Jews in the Holocaust was wrong? In fact, the Nazis offered that very argument as a defense at the Nuremberg trials. They argued, 'How can you come from another culture and condemn what we did when our culture said it was acceptable?' In condemning them, the world said that there is something beyond culture, above culture, that determines right and wrong."

My dad was teaching me a powerful point: *If indeed all values are relative to individual cultures, then the world court had no right to judge the Nazis as wrong*. This is the great failure of moral relativism. The Nazis were not judged by American law or European law, but by natural law, by universal law. The trial assumed that a universal, objective, and constant moral law really exists. And as we will see, only the existence of God can account for such an absolute, universal law.

THE IMPOSSIBILITY OF LIVING AS A RELATIVIST

You Can't Steal My Stereo!

One afternoon my former professor J. P. Moreland shared the gospel with a student at the University of Vermont. The student began to espouse moral relativism. He said, "Whatever is true for you is true for you, and whatever is true for me is true for me. If something works for you because you believe it, that's great. But no one should force his or her views on other people since everything is relative."[3]

J. P. knew that if he allowed the student to get away with his moral relativism, he could never understand the nature of sin, which is breaking the objective moral commands of God. And if there could be for him no such thing as real, objective sin measured against the objective moral command of God, why would he need a Savior? So J. P. thanked the student for his time and began to leave his room. But on the way out J. P. picked up the student's small stereo and began to walk out with it.

"Hey, what are you doing?!" he shouted.

"What's wrong with you?" replied J. P. "Are you having problems with your eyes? I am leaving your room with your stereo."

"You can't do that," he gushed.

"Well," J. P. replied, "since I lift weights and jog regularly, I think I can in fact do it without any help. But maybe you meant to say, 'You *ought* not do that because you are stealing my stereo.' Of course, I know from our previous conversation that this is not what you mean. I happen to think it is permissible to steal stereos if it will help a person's religious devotions, and I myself could use a stereo to listen to Christian music in my morning devotions. Now I would never try to force you to accept my moral beliefs in this regard because, as you said, everything is relative and we shouldn't force our ideas on others. But surely you aren't going to force on me your belief that it is wrong to steal your stereo, are you?" The student quickly realized the inconsistency in his thinking. He had no basis for stopping J. P. from stealing his stereo if "everything is relative."

Everyone in the Class Fails!

Professor Peter Kreeft had an entire college class who told him that morality was relative, and that he had no right to impose his values of absolutism on them. So he replied, "All right. Let's run the class by your values, not mine. There are no absolutes. Moral values are subjective and relative. And my particular set of subjective personal moral values includes this one: All women in my class flunk!" Immediately the students protested:

"That's unfair!"

"Yes, it is unfair," Kreeft agreed. "But what do you mean by 'fair'? If fairness, or justice, is only MY value or YOUR value, then it has no universal authority over both of us. I have no right to impose MY values on you, and you have no right to impose yours on me. But if there is a universal, objective, absolute value called justice, or fairness, then it holds for both of us, and it judges me as wrong when I say all women flunk. And you can appeal to that justice in judging my rule as unfair. But if there is no such thing as absolute objective justice, then all you can mean when you protest my rule is that you don't like it, that your subjective values are different from mine. But that's not what you said. You didn't say merely that you don't like my rules, but that it was unfair. So you do believe in moral absolutes after all, when it comes down to practice. Why do you believe that silly theory, then? Why are you hypocrites? Why don't you practice what you preach and stop appealing to justice, or else preach what you practice, and stop denying it."[4]

These two stories point out an undeniable truth: *Moral relativism is unlivable*. The young man was willing to be a moral relativist when it was convenient for him, but he quickly became a moral absolutist as soon as someone attempted to steal his stereo. The students in Dr. Kreeft's class espoused relativism until it involved their own grades, and then they quickly cried out for an objective standard!

THREE MORE PROBLEMS FOR RELATIVISM

Disagreement Is Overrated

Moral relativism, the view that all values are determined by each unique culture or individual, does *seem* to be born out of different cultural perspectives. There is no absolute moral obligation to drive on the right side of the road. That obligation is true relative to America but not to England. Many people who live in India will not eat cattle, but few in the U.S. pass up a good burger. Some people think homosexuality is moral, while others do not. From the fashions of local dress to the dicta of people's ethics, there seems to be great variety across cultures. But is this the whole story?

What proponents of moral relativism fail to realize is that *there is far more similarity across cultures than difference*. For example, every society has some version of the Golden Rule. While some societies say a man may have four wives, no culture says he may simply take any woman he wants. All societies have laws protecting human life, all condemn stealing, all honor courage, and all say that engaging in sexual acts with anyone is not permitted. It's as if many different orchestras are performing the same musical piece but adapting the harmonics to fit their own instruments.

A modern example where disagreement is overrated can be found in the abortion debate. Here's the conventional wisdom: the issue of abortion involves two sides with totally opposing value systems. But much of the time both sides hold their primary values in common. After all, most pro-choice and pro-life people share the belief that all human persons possess certain alienable rights as stated in the Declaration of Independence. Usually they don't disagree about whether full human beings have basic rights but about who qualifies as a full human being. Many pro-choice advocates believe human beings have certain basic rights, but they deny that fetuses are full human beings. And many pro-life advocates believe in a woman's right to choose; they just believe that choice is limited in the case of abortion by the rights of the unborn baby. So there really is more agreement here than many people think. There's an agreement about values but a disagreement about facts—an agreement about principles but a disagreement about how to apply those principles.

We also sometimes ignore the fact that there are a large number of issues on which the majority of North Americans agree (e.g., it is wrong to torture babies for fun, to molest five-year-old children, to commit rape). And there also are a great number of past moral conflicts that have been solved (e.g., slavery, women's rights, child labor). While there is some disagreement on moral issues, as moral relativists often claim, we must not overlook the great amount of common ground.

The Fatal Flaw of Relativism

Like the claim "There is no truth," the philosophy of moral relativism is self-contradictory. The proponent of moral relativism says that there are no absolute truths that apply to all people, in all places, for all times, so people *ought* to follow their personal or cultural values. But upon closer analysis we realize that the relativist is making an absolute claim, namely, that everyone *ought* to be a relativist and follow their personal or cultural norms. So on one hand the relativist says there are no absolute truths, but on the other hand the relativist holds relativism as being absolutely true. Thus, *no one can hold moral relativism without being inconsistent.* This is why Dr. Norman Geisler has observed, "Moral absolutes are unavoidable. Those who deny them use them."[5] In fact, it is impossible to deny the existence of absolutes without appealing to an absolute.

Relativism Is a Close-minded and Intolerant View

Tolerance, throughout the history of Western civilization, meant to recognize and respect someone's beliefs without sharing them. In other words, you only had tolerance for someone you did not agree with. But today's definition of tolerance is radically different. Tolerance today means that *everyone is equally right*. That is why people are labeled as "intolerant" for claiming to have the correct or right view on a moral issue.

Many people see relativism as necessary for promoting tolerance, nonjudgmentalism, and inclusiveness, for they think if a person is convinced his or her moral position is right and others' wrong, then that person is closed-minded and intolerant. But in reality, relativism by its own standards is itself a close-minded and intolerant position. After all, the relativist asserts *uncompromisingly* that there is no moral truth. Consider the following discussion between a high-school student and her teacher:

The teacher instructs her class, "Welcome, students. This is the first day of class, and so I want to lay down some ground rules. First, since no one has the truth about morality, you should be open-minded to the opinions of your fellow students." The teacher recognizes the hand of Elizabeth, who asks, "If nobody has the truth, isn't it a good reason for me *not* to listen to my fellow students? After all, if nobody has the truth, why should I waste my time listening to other people and their opinions? What's the point? Only if somebody has the truth does it make sense to be open-minded. Don't you agree?"

The teacher responded, "No, I don't. Are you claiming to know the truth? Isn't that a bit arrogant and dogmatic?"

"Not at all. Rather, I think it's dogmatic, as well as arrogant, to assert that no single person on earth knows the truth. After all, have you met every person in the world and quizzed them exhaustively? If not, how can you make such a claim? Also, I believe it is actually the opposite of arrogance to say that I will alter my opinions to fit the truth whenever and wherever I find it. And if I happen to think that I have good reason to believe I do know the truth and would like to share it with you, why wouldn't you listen to me? Why would you automatically discredit my opinion before it is even uttered? I thought we were supposed to listen to everyone's opinion?"[6]

This girl made a very profound point: *Those who preach tolerance are often the most intolerant*. If moral relativists were truly inclusive and tolerant, wouldn't they be accepting of those who believe morals are objective? But clearly they are not. Christians are not the only ones who may deserve the label "intolerant," for moral relativists are just as exclusive to views that differ from their own.

GOD ON THE STAGE

Moral relativism clearly fails as an explanation for human morality. Given its failure, it seems reasonable to ask, "Is there a more solid base for morality?" Let's consider the two most popular explanations for morality.

The Social Contract Theory

This theory says that laws are the result of a social contract among consenting adults. In other words, people got together and created laws so they could survive and function as a race. It's as if we came together and created moral rules based on the dictum "If you scratch my back, I'll scratch yours." Despite its popularity, the social contract theory has *four* key problems:

1. There is no rational basis for asking the minority to give up his wants for the sake of the majority. Why should the minority care about the majority? Why should you care about the benefit of the group if it doesn't in turn help you?
2. When individuals reject the social contract we are left with what philosopher Friedrich Nietzsche called "the will to power." In other words, those in power determine morality—might makes right.
3. If someone can escape the consequences of a social contract, then why should his/her behavior be considered objectively wrong?
4. We intrinsically know that certain actions are right (such as helping the poor) and that certain actions are wrong (torturing babies for fun). We don't need a social contract to know the intrinsic rightness and wrongness of certain actions.

The Instinct Theory of Morality

According to this theory the process of *evolution* accounts for the universal moral code. We have a sense of right and wrong because *nature* gave it to us. There are *three* key problems with such an approach to ethics:

1. According to the instinct theory we should obey nature; but before we can obey nature, it seems we ought to ask *which* nature we should obey. We all have conflicting urges. Sometimes we feel the desire to help people, yet sometimes we have the urge to hurt people. If nature gave us both urges, then isn't it strange to applaud one yet discount the other? We are left with no basis for determining which nature we ought to follow.
2. If nature gave us our sense of morality to preserve the human race, then wouldn't certain actions—such as rape—be right if they helped me to pass on my genes to the next generation? If I were the strongest to survive, then what is wrong with my

actions? Yet we all know that rape is wrong regardless of the circumstances.

3. If our sense of morality comes from nature, then why isn't it more natural? If morality were merely an instinct that evolved like our instinct for food or our instinct for survival, then morality would be as natural for us as it is for salmon to swim upstream or for geese to fly south in the winter. Wouldn't we do right naturally without even thinking about it?

It seems that moral relativism, the social contract theory, as well as the instinct theory all fail to account for morality. So what possibly could be the foundation for right and wrong?

God on the Stage

Back in the days of Julius Caesar, there was a Roman poet and playwright named Horace. Horace criticized the laziness of many playwrights of his day. He strongly criticized those writers who, every time a problem occurred in the plot of their play, brought in one of the many Roman gods to solve it. Horace instructed, "Do not bring a god on to the stage unless the problem is one that deserves a god to solve it."

The challenge of finding a foundation for ethics is one that deserves—in fact, demands—a God to solve it. All other foundations, as we have seen, fail. It is impossible to arrive at an objective, universal, and constant standard of truth and morality without bringing God onto the stage. In *The Brothers Karamazov,* Russian novelist Fyodor Dostoyevsky aptly observed, "If there is no God, all is permissible." In other words, if God does not exist as the foundation of morality, then *anything goes*. If God does not exist then we lose the right to judge the Nazis and anyone else with whom we disagree morally. If there is no greater source above human beings, then the existence of morality is an inexplicable illusion.

Yet if God exists, then we have reason to believe in morality. We *ought* to be truthful, because God is truth. We *ought* to do loving acts, because God is love. Morality stems from the character and nature of God and is binding on his creation. The existence of morality points to the absolute of God's existence and character. Only God's existence and character can properly account for morality. So how do we know God exists?

THE EXISTENCE OF GOD

British intellectual G. K. Chesterton once compared God to the sun: We cannot look at it directly, but without it we cannot see anything. There are some powerful arguments for the existence of God. Consider a brief description of a few:[7]

1. ***The argument from a first cause.*** Everything that begins to exist must have a cause. Since science and philosophy have demonstrated that the universe began to exist some time in the past, we must ask the logical question, what caused it? One explanation is to claim that everything in existence literally came from *nothing* and by chance. But the more reasonable explanation is to conclude that there is an eternal cause outside of space and time that brought the universe into existence, namely God.
2. ***The argument from design.*** Whenever we see design in the world we postulate a designer. For example, if I come home and find the dinner table set I naturally infer that someone (most likely my wife) set the table. Similarly, the universe itself bears the marks of design. Because the earth is so *perfectly* fit for human life (the distance from the sun, the existence of water, the percentage of oxygen in the atmosphere, etc.), it is natural to postulate a Designer.
3. ***The argument from morality.*** Every human culture known to man has had a moral law. While there are some disagreements across cultures, there also are striking similarities. Without appeal to a higher source, namely God, what could account for the common sense of morality in the entire human race throughout all of history? Where else could morals have come from?
4. ***The argument from information***—information requires an information-giver. Whenever we find an ordered display of information in the world, we infer that it came from a mind, not chance. We know that a book, since it has orderly information, must have had an author. Interestingly, we find a vast array of ordered information encoded in the human body. For example, there is more information in a single cell than three or four entire sets of the *Encyclopedia Britannica!* DNA carries information, which is why

scientists use the letters A-C-T-G to describe its content. Therefore, we must ask, who is the information-giver for the great quantity of information in the human body?

5. ***Argument from the resurrection of Jesus Christ***—the entire Christian movement is based on a single historical fact: Jesus rose from the dead on the third day (1 Cor. 15:3–17). This is not a mere belief of blind faith, but one rooted in the critical analysis of history. Skeptics have tried to explain away the resurrection, but none have been successful. Jesus rose from the dead, and this is one powerful piece of evidence that attests to the existence of God.

ONE FINAL QUESTION: WHO ARE WE TO JUDGE?

One of the most commonly misquoted verses today is Matthew 7:1. I often hear students quote this verse with an air of superiority: "Do not judge lest you be judged." Since Jesus said not to judge, who are we to disobey? But as with any other verse in the Bible, we must look at the *context* for a proper interpretation.

The greater context of Matthew 7:1 is the Sermon on the Mount, where Jesus talks to his followers (not nonbelievers) about living for the kingdom of God. We need to recognize that when Jesus condemned judging, he wasn't implying we should never make moral judgments about people. After all, just a few verses later Jesus calls certain people "pigs" and "dogs" and "wolves in sheep's clothing"! (Matt. 7:6, 15) What Jesus rebukes is *hypocritical* judgment, where we judge others with a standard we refuse to apply to ourselves. Sometimes judging is OK, but to judge hypocritically is wrong. This is precisely why Jesus said, "Do not judge according to appearance, but judge with righteous judgment" (John 7:24). While it is right to judge actions such as cheating or sexual promiscuity as wrong, we have no right to consider ourselves better than others. And when we judge we are to make a righteous judgment rather than rely on our preferences or prejudices. Consider some other verses in Matthew where Jesus commands his followers to make judgments:

Matthew 7:15–20	Jesus' followers are commanded to make a *judgment* regarding those who claim to be prophets.
Matthew 10:11–15	Jesus commands his followers to make *judgments* about households they visit on evangelistic outings.
Matthew 16:6–12	Jesus' followers are to make *judgments* regarding the teachings of the Pharisees and Sadducees.
Matthew 18:15–17	Jesus' disciples are commanded to make *judgments* regarding the actions of brothers caught in sin.

To be judgmental should not mean "to disagree with someone," or "to consider someone morally wrong." For even the relativist considers the absolutist to be wrong. Being judgmental should be correctly understood as *thinking we are better than other people because of their moral failures.* Such an attitude is inconsistent with the biblical command to love one another (1 John 4:7), for God is the one who ultimately judges the heart (1 Sam. 16:7).

HOW SHOULD WE RESPOND?

Act in Love, Not Arrogance

Making moral judgments does not necessarily make someone arrogant—if it is done in love. Mother Theresa demonstrated this in a speech she gave at a national prayer breakfast in 1994. She boldly condemned abortion before the pro-choice president and vice-president of the United States. Although she spoke in a respectful manner, she made powerful statements in defense of unborn babies: "And if we accept that a mother can kill even her own child, how can we tell other people not to kill one another? Any country that accepts abortion is not teaching its people to love, but to use any violence to get what they want."[8] Because of her bold commitment to the poor and downtrodden, nobody accused this nun of arrogance. Likewise, when we act with *genuine love* it is very difficult for people to label us as arrogant, intolerant, and judgmental.

Recognize Fallacious Thinking

Frank Beckwith recently participated in a discussion panel with people from all political and religious persuasions over the moral responsibility of the media. At one point during his speech a young woman raised her hand and asked him, "Who are you to judge?" She was implying that he had no right to make moral judgments about the actions of others. Frank gave this reply, "I am a rational person who is aware of certain fundamental principles of logic and moral reasoning. I think I'm qualified. Would you rather have animals judge?" His response absolutely shocked her. He was making the point that we *do* have the right to make moral judgments, in fact that is one key difference between humans and animals. Having a moral conscience and making moral judgments are parts of being human.

Frank went on to say, "Your claim that I have no right to make judgments is itself a judgment about me. Your claim, therefore, is self-contradictory."[9] Anyone who says you should not judge has already made a moral judgment about you, namely that you are *wrong* for judging others. Next time someone says, "Who are you to judge?" you might reply by asking, "Who are you to ask the question, who are you to judge?"

Turn the Tables

If you find yourself in a situation where you suspect your beliefs will be labeled judgmental, intolerant, exclusive, and narrow-minded, *turn the tables*. When someone asks for your personal views about a moral issue, you might respond boldly, yet lovingly with the following question: "You know, this is actually a very personal question you're asking, and I'd be glad to answer. But before I do, I want to know if you consider yourself a tolerant or an intolerant person. Is it safe to give my opinion, or are you going to judge me for my point of view? Do you respect diverse points of view, or do you condemn others for convictions that differ from yours?"[10]

Then when you give your viewpoint, it will be quite difficult for someone to call you intolerant or judgmental without also looking guilty. This response capitalizes on the fact that *there is no such thing as moral neutrality*. Everybody has a point of view they think is right, and everybody makes moral judgments on a regular basis. The Christian gets labeled as the judgmental one, but everyone else judges too. It's an inescapable consequence of standing for morality.

CONCLUSION

Moral relativism is a myth that has been pulled over the eyes of your generation. Despite its overwhelming popularity, relativism is riddled with serious problems. It is unable to account for the moral compass across cultures, and it leaves one in a position unable to make moral judgments (i.e., "Who are you to judge the Nazis for actions their culture concluded were right?"). It is only when we embrace God as the foundation for ethics that we can make moral judgments.

Review

1. What are the primary differences between relativism and absolutism?
2. What was the point of the conversation I had with my dad about *Schindler's List*? What shortfall does it highlight regarding relativism?
3. Why is it impossible to live as a relativist? Explain the points of the two stories "You can't steal my stereo!" and "Everyone in the class fails."
4. Describe the three additional problems for relativism.
5. Describe the following two theories of morality and their corresponding weaknesses:
   Social Contract Theory
   The Instinct Theory
6. Summarize the five basic arguments for the existence of God.
7. How can we respond to the question, "Who are you to judge?"

Small Group Discussion

1. Discuss the following quote by Fyodor Dostoyevsky: "If there is no God, all is permissible." What does this mean? Do you agree or disagree? Why is there no ultimate accountability for human action if God does not exist?
2. Have you ever been called judgmental, arrogant, or intolerant? Do many Christians deserve these labels? What can we do in conversation and lifestyle to avoid such labels, so our views can be heard fairly?given by Jesus. Why do you think we can find happiness only when we stop focusing so much on ourselves?

The Morality of Sex

PURPOSE

To understand the biblical reasons behind God's precepts regarding sexual immorality and learn why people who follow his plan are among the most sexually satisfied people on the face of the earth

In this chapter you will learn

- That the principles of love, purity, and faithfulness are behind God's commands about sex, which are in turn supported by God's own character
- The three primary purposes of sex
- The truth about STDs, condoms, pornography, and oral sex
- Four reasons why people who follow God's plan are experiencing the most fulfilling sex lives
- Tips for winning the battle of sexual purity
- How to be restored to spiritual and emotional virginity

There is a sexual revolution going on among your generation. But despite what the media might say, this is not a sexual revolution against traditional values like the generation of the 1960s. This revolution is radically different. In fact, this revolution consists of young people like you, who are sick and tired of being bombarded with false information about sex. You have seen too many people get hurt, too many scarred lives, and too many broken hearts. You want to take a stand for the truth. A recent *Newsweek* article put it this way: "There's a sexual revolution going on in America. . . . Rejecting the get-down-make-love ethos of their parents' generation, this wave of young adults represents a new counterculture, one clearly at odds with the mainstream media and their routine use of sex to boost ratings and peddle product. . . . More teens are saying, 'no.'"[1]

Despite the fact that your generation is demanding real answers about sex, *you have, in today's sex-saturated culture, more hurdles to overcome to take a stand for righteousness than any generation in history*. You can hardly turn on the TV, browse the Internet, watch a movie, or walk down the street without getting bombarded with a counterfeit message about sexuality. In fact, it's been said that the typical teenager today faces more pressures in the area of sex on his way to the bus stop than his grandpa did on Friday night when he was out looking for it!

So, who can possibly expect a young man or a young woman to take a stand for sexual purity today? The answer to this question is simple: God does. His standards haven't changed, even if ours have. St. Thomas More once said, "The times are *never* so bad that a good man cannot live in them." Times are clearly bad, but this is no excuse for making poor choices. As the author of Hebrews proclaimed, God will "equip you in every good thing to do His will" (13:21). Are you up for the challenge?

WHAT DOES GOD HAVE TO SAY ABOUT SEX?

The Precepts

Most young people are familiar with the *precepts* of the Bible, which are God's commands regarding sexual behavior:

- "You are to abstain from . . . sexual immorality" (Acts 15:29 NIV).
- "Flee from sexual immorality" (1 Cor. 6:18 NIV).
- "But among you there must not be even a hint of sexual immorality" (Eph. 5:3 NIV).
- "Put to death, therefore, whatever belongs to your earthly nature: sexual immorality, impurity, lust, evil desires" (Col. 3:5 NIV).

The Principles

But most young people are unfamiliar with *why* God gave us such commands. God's precepts are not designed to steal our fun or to make us miserable. Rather, they are designed to protect us and to provide for us the greatest blessings imaginable. Behind God's precepts about sexuality are three *principles*: love, purity, and faithfulness.

Love provides the foundation for biblical sex. So many young people today believe that "love makes it right." In fact, teens say that love is even a greater determinate than whether they could have sex with the assurance that they wouldn't get caught (which may surprise some because not getting caught is very appealing to many young people!). I happen to agree that "love makes it right." But before you start a book-burning crusade with this book, let me make my case. You see, love makes it right because love is necessarily self*less*, not self*ish*. Love looks out for the betterment of the other instead of oneself. True love would not engage in an activity that could possibly harm someone or lead another to sin. True love, as my dad shared with me, is *when the happiness, health, and spiritual growth of another person are as important to you as your own* (see Eph. 5:33). True love focuses on giving, not taking. The real lover says, "I will love you . . . period." This type of love is only possible within the commitment of marriage. And it is this type of love that "makes it right."

Purity provides the foundation for biblical sex. In the movie *Meet the Parents*, Greg Focker (played by Ben Stiller) plays a star-crossed lover eager to earn the approval of his potential in-laws. Robert DeNiro, who plays Greg's potential father-in-law, talks about a "circle of trust" that is reserved only for those close to the family. This circle of trust, once it is broken, can never be mended. Similarly, the sexual union between a man and a woman is meant to form an unbroken circle, a pure union: two virgins entering into an undivided relationship. Hebrews 13:4 says, "Marriage should be honored by all, and the marriage bed kept *pure*" (NIV). That circle, that union, can be broken even *before* marriage, if one or both partners have not kept the marriage bed pure by reserving sex for the proper context of marriage.

Faithfulness provides the foundation for biblical sex. The biblical standard for sex demands that two people remain faithful to each other in a lifelong commitment. This is the reason the psalmist said, "Love and faithfulness meet together" (Ps. 85:10 NIV). This is why marriage is so pivotal for biblical sexuality, because it provides the necessary platform for a lifetime of commitment. For love to truly flourish, it requires faithfulness.

The Person

God's precepts for human sexuality are based on the biblical principles of love, purity, and faithfulness. Those principles, in turn, are based upon the *person* of God himself.

God is love. Love is not merely an action God performs; it is who God *is*. The Bible states, "God is love, and the one who abides in love abides in God, and God abides in him" (1 John 4:16). Because God *is* love, he always *acts* lovingly. This love is what motivated God to send his only son to suffer and die for us. And this is why we are commanded to "not love with word or with tongue, but in deed and truth" (1 John 3:18).

God is pure. God does not just command his people to be pure, but God *is* pure in his very character and nature (1 John 3:3). God has no spots, blemishes, or pollutions—he is completely pure. Even God's words are perfectly pure (Ps. 12:6; James 3:17). He demonstrated his purity to his people: he demanded the use of *pure* gold in the ark and temple; he prescribed *pure* incense in worship; he expected *pure* animals for sacrifice; he demanded *pure* hearts (Matt. 5:8), *pure* religion (James 1:27), and *pure* relationships (1 Tim. 5:2). And when God took on a human nature, in the person of Jesus Christ, he offered the most *pure* sacrifice possible—himself!

God is faithful. "The Rock! His work is perfect, for all His ways are just," cried Moses to the Israelites as they prepared to enter the Promised Land. "A God of *faithfulness* and without injustice, righteous and upright is He" (Deut. 32:4). The same God who was faithful to Moses is still faithful to his people today. "If we are faithless," writes Paul, "He remains faithful, for He cannot deny Himself" (2 Tim. 2:13). In other words, God cannot be unfaithful, for he is faithful in his very character and nature. And this is why even God's words are "faithful and true" (Rev. 21:5).

Most young people are well aware of the biblical precepts regarding sexuality. But in everyday situations, especially in the midst of temptation, they begin to wonder if those precepts are still applicable today. However, when we determine the principles behind the precepts and then allow them to point us to the person of God, we can see that the standards of the Bible are just as true and relevant today as they ever were. This is because they are not human standards subject to error and change, but are established in the very character and nature of God—the God in whom "there is no variation or shifting shadow" (James 1:17). The Word of God makes it clear that chastity—biblical love, sexual purity, and marital faithfulness—is right for all people, at all times, and in all places.[2]

THE PURPOSE OF SEX

Not too long ago I called my Internet service provider for help with my home computer. Right before hanging up I decided to ask the operator a simple question (you should try this some time!). I said, "What are the craziest questions you have ever received from people on how to use a computer?" He gave me the following hilarious responses. One lady asked for help on how to use the foot pedal on her computer. Can you guess what she was using? The mouse! Another young man said the cupholder on his computer was too small to hold his favorite mug. What do you think he was using as a cupholder? You probably guessed it—he was trying to use his CD-ROM drive! And another lady walked around her house closing all the open windows because the computer screen said "Close all open windows."

We may laugh at these honest mistakes because we recognize their failure to properly understand a computer. The mouse is not meant to function as a foot pedal, and the CD-ROM is not designed to hold cups. The computer is designed to function in a certain manner, and when it is not used in that manner, frustration often results.

This same principle applies to sexuality. The rules of sexual morality are not merely devised by men, but by God. They are not random rules meant to steal our fun, but are based on the nature of man and the nature of God. The rule "Flee sexual immorality" is similar to the rule "Thou shall not eat fatty foods" in dieting or "Thou shall do thy homework" in school. No matter how hard you believe, fatty foods will not make you healthy. And no matter how smart you are, you have to do your homework to succeed in school (if not now, you will have to in college!). Philosopher Peter Kreeft puts it this way: "Christian sexual morality, like the rest of morality, is based on human nature, on the kind of thing we are and the kind of thing sex is. It is not the changeable rules of a game we designed but the unchangeable rules of the operating manual written by the designer of our human nature."[3]

Some people hold that sex is merely the fulfillment of a natural, animal desire that we have inherited from our evolutionary ancestors. The purpose of sex, in this view, is merely to pass on one's genes to the next generation to foster the "survival of the species." But this view is greatly mistaken. According to God—the creator of sex—there are three primary purposes for sexuality. And when we ignore these purposes, just as when we ignore the instructions on how to properly use a computer, there will be consequences. So what is the purpose of sex?

1. Procreation. It hardly comes as a surprise to hear that one of the primary purposes of sex is to make babies. In Genesis 1:28, God said to the first human couple: "Be fruitful and multiply, and fill the earth." Interestingly, what most people don't realize is that God gave a *command* for people to have kids, not just a suggestion. This is a command I do not hear anyone complaining about!

2. Unity. One of the most powerful aspects of sex is its ability to bond people together. The writer of Genesis says, "This explains why a man leaves his father and mother and is joined to his wife, and the two are *united* into one" (2:24 NLT). Sex is not merely a physical act; it also involves an emotional, relational, and spiritual connection. Sex bonds people in the most intimate way. That is why it is so difficult for some teenagers to break up after being involved sexually.

3. Recreation. So many people think God is a cosmic killjoy when it comes to sexuality. But what they fail to realize is that God is the one who made sex so fun in the first place! In fact, God could have made procreation boring and provincial, but instead he made it one of the most exhilarating human experiences in the world. Proverbs 5:18-19 says, "Let your fountain be blessed, and rejoice in the wife of your youth. As a loving hind and a graceful doe, let her breasts satisfy you at all times; be exhilarated always with her love." God designed sex to be enjoyable, but sadly so many young people today, rather than holding out for God's best, are settling for a second-rate experience.

THE TRUTH ABOUT SEX

Have you ever had a toy that you truly loved? My favorite toy in fourth grade was my Optimus-Prime Transformer. Optimus-Prime was the leader of the Autobots in their battle against the evil Decepticons. In the cartoon, Optimus-Prime could transform instantly from a man-like machine into an eighteen-wheel truck. But, to my frustration, it always took me a bit longer to transform the characters in real life than they took in the cartoon.

But then I saw a commercial that changed my view forever. There were finally Transformers that would change themselves! Wow! I was so excited to get the new auto-Transformers I could hardly contain myself! All you had to do was wind them up, let them go, and then they would transform just like the cartoon. So I saved up my money and ordered one by mail. I could hardly wait for the day when my package would arrive. But to my great disappointment, it was not nearly as "cool" as the commercial had indicated. It was slower, smaller, and made more cheaply than I had expected. Despite my initial excitement and anticipation, I had been duped.

This is much like what happens to young people today in the area of sex. There is so much "false advertising" about sex, and sadly, many young people are buying right into the lies. The media, educational system, and many of our friends have ideas about how sex should be; but few know the truth. This is powerfully illustrated in a recent conversation a young girl had with the editors of *Seventeen* magazine.[4]

- ***A young girl:*** "I was diagnosed with HPV (Human Papillomavirus). I've had the warts removed, but will the virus make me and my boyfriend infertile?"
- ***Seventeen magazine:*** "Some people, of course, get freaked out by having warts in their vaginal area, but generally they're nothing more than a nuisance. In rare cases, these strains can cause cancer of the cervix, vulva, or vagina. One comforting thought is that you are hardly alone. An estimated 20 million people, including 1/3 of all sexually active teenagers, have HPV. All this may sound depressing, but don't worry too much. While there is no cure yet for HPV, there are many treatments for those unpleasant warts. In the future, you should always use a condom."

This article—like much of the message young people receive about sexuality—is riddled with misinformation. For one thing, genital warts are far more than a nuisance. In fact, they are extremely common. Genital warts can occur in the vaginal area, on the penis or cervix, or near the anus. And sadly, babies who are exposed to them during childbirth may get warts in the throat.

Even though only 11 percent of teenagers are familiar with HPV, it is by far the most common sexually transmitted disease (STD). As many as 45 million Americans are already infected with HPV, more than twice as many as mentioned by *Seventeen* magazine.[5] The Medical Institute for Sexual Health estimates that 33 percent of all women are infected with HPV.[6] Among young women under the age of twenty-five, studies have found that between 28 and 46 percent are typically infected with HPV.[7] One study at Rutgers University showed that 60 percent of sexually active women tested positive for HPV at least some time during the three-year study.[8]

HPV has far greater consequences than genital warts: it causes cancer. HPV is the cause of more than 90 percent of all cervical cancer, the second most common cancer among women in the United

States.[9] In fact, cervical cancer caused by HPV kills more women in the United States than AIDS. I challenge you to give this serious thought.

WHEN CRUNCH TIME COMES, WE MAKE CHOICES BASED UPON WHAT WE TRULY BELIEVE.

What about Condoms?

But what about using a condom (as *Seventeen* suggests)? The National Institutes of Health states: "Condoms provide almost no protection against HPV."[10] The reason is because HPV (and many other STDs) are passed through skin-to-skin contact in areas that are not covered by a condom. The bottom line for condoms is this: *even if they are used accurately and consistently* (which rarely happens for youth) *they succeed in only decreasing the risks, not eliminating them*.

This is why an *American College of Obstetricians and Gynecologists Newsletter* referred to condoms as "an antiquated system of birth control," going on to say, "Condoms often do not prevent sexually transmitted disease. Each year 25 percent of women whose partners use condoms for contraception get pregnant."[11] Condoms are a poor way to practice "safe sex." They often break, slip, leak, and some viruses are so microscopically small they find their way through the pores in the material.[12]

There is only one method for preventing the consequences of premarital sex: *abstinence* until marriage. The Medical Institute for Sexual Health defines abstinence as "the calculated decision and deliberate action to refrain from sexual activity." Sexual activity is "any activity that involves intentional contact for the purpose of sexual arousal."[13] Such activity includes sexual intercourse, heavy petting, oral sex, mutual masturbation, and other purposeful sexual touching.

THE CASE FOR A BIBLICAL VIEW OF SEX

There is a powerful myth going around about Christians and sex. The myth is that Christians are missing out on all the fun. Fred Berger, former professor at the University of California Davis, explains: "The fact is that most sex is routinized, dull, unfulfilling . . . precisely because its practice is governed by the restraints the conservatives [Christians] insist on. Those constraints dictate with *whom* one has sex, *when* one has sex, how *often* one has sex, *where* one has sex and so on."[14] In other words, Christians spoil all the fun because they have so many rules about sexual conduct.

An article entitled "Aha! Call It the Revenge of the Church Ladies," appeared not too long ago in *USA Today* and helped to debunk this myth.[15] The author of the article, William R. Mattox Jr., compiled the results from the largest and most accurate sex surveys ever conducted. He wanted to know who is having the *best* sex and who is having the *most* sex. This is what he concluded based on the data: *Church ladies (and the men who sleep with them) are among the most sexually satisfied people on the face of the earth*. Religious women, according to the study, experience *significantly* higher levels of sexual satisfaction than non-religious women. He concludes his article by saying, "Now these religious teachings are apt to come as a shock to those who believe God is a cosmic killjoy when it comes to sexuality." The author said, "Nevertheless, the common assumption continues to be that church ladies are sexually repressed, or that they're like the blissfully ignorant women of *Pleasantville* who think they've got it good but have no idea what they are missing." Despite the popularity of this myth, he cites four reasons why Christians are having *far* better sex than those who reject God's plan:

1. Saving Sex for Marriage Pays Considerable Dividends

One of the myths of our society seems to be that in order to make informed decisions about sex, you have to first experience it. But studies show the exact opposite! Here are what the facts show: *The more you preserve yourself sexually before marriage, the greater satisfaction you will have with your future spouse in marriage*. The *USA Today* article put it this way: "Several studies show that women who engage in early sexual activity and those who have had multiple partners are less apt to express satisfaction with their sex lives than women who entered marriage with little or no sexual baggage." So true!

When teenagers choose to be involved in prolonged kissing, heavy petting, and oral sex, they are robbing themselves of future intimacy with their spouses. This is why the New Testament is so clear in its condemnation of fornication (i.e., sexual activity before marriage).[16] Sexual relationships *before* marriage destroy God's purposes *in* marriage. But choosing to save sexual activity for marriage will provide immeasurable blessing. In his best-seller *I Loved a Girl*, Walter Trobisch reinforces this biblical truth: "When I as a pastor am called to counsel in a marriage crisis, I can almost always trace the origin of the problems to the kind of life which the husband and wife lived before they were married. The young man who has not learned self-control before marriage will not have it during marriage. . . . In a sense, you deprive your future wife of something, even if you do not yet know her, and you endanger your happiness together."[17]

2. People Benefit from Committing to Marital Permanence

Kids say the funniest things! In a recent *National Review* article, some "Young Scholars," ages 7–8, were asked to describe well-known Bible stories. Here are some of my favorite responses:

- "Adam and Eve were created from an apple tree."
- "Noah's wife was called Joan of Ark."
- "Moses led the Hebrews to the Red Sea, where they made un-leavened bread, which is bread made without any ingredients."
- "Moses died before he ever reached Canada."
- "Solomon, one of David's sons, had 300 wives and 700 porcupines."
- "Jesus enunciated the Golden Rule, which says to do unto others before they do unto you."

- "A Christian should have only one spouse. This is called *monotony.*"[18]

Sadly, this last "scholarly observation" portrays how our culture and many young people feel about marriage—that being stuck with one person for life brings boredom and monotony. But this is so far from the truth! According to the *USA Today* article mentioned earlier, "Most major studies show a *strong* correlation between monogamous marriage and sexual satisfaction."

In other words, being committed to one person for life will actually benefit you in your sexuality! Why? Because sexual enjoyment flourishes in the midst of a committed relationship. When you are able to get to know someone with true intimacy, sex becomes far more than merely a pleasurable physical activity. Rather, it becomes a sacred connection of two souls on the deepest level imaginable. And when two souls are committed together in such a union, the pleasures of sex can be indescribable. Such an experience can take place only within the context of marriage.

3. God's Plan Offers Far Greater Sexual Freedom

Although it may be a difficult concept to grasp at first, following God's rules for sexuality actually provides the greatest amount of freedom. How is this possible? Let me explain. One of my friends recently took his junior high youth group to play paintball. On the way home a seventh grader named Johnny spoke up and said, "That was awesome! I loved the strategy of the game, but most of all I loved shooting at people and the rush of dodging bullets. In fact, when I'm older I want to go to war!"

An older youth worker, who had been in war, spoke up and said to Johnny, "You are missing the point. You see, paintball is fun because there are no consequences for your actions. You might get hit with a paintball and at most you will have a welt. In paintball, you are *free* to play the game without any inhibitions because there is *no fear*. But in war, there are extreme consequences and there is great fear. If you get hit, it just might cost you your life."

Sex in marriage can be compared to playing a game of paintball—you are free to enjoy yourself without fear of negative consequences. If you both have followed God's plan for purity, then you don't have to worry about a broken condom, being rejected, contracting a sexually transmitted disease, or having to deal with the issue of abortion. When we ignore God's plan we are riddled with anxiety because of the real and stressful consequences. This is why the *USA Today* article stated: "Part of the reason church ladies are having so much fun is that they don't have to worry about many of the fears commonly associated with sexual promiscuity, such as AIDS and other sexually transmitted diseases, pregnancy, fear of rejection and fear of getting caught."

There is so much confusion over the nature of freedom in your generation. An alcoholic once said to me, "This is America. I am free to drink if I like." I simply replied, "Are you free *not* to drink?" He was silent. Young people think they are free to look at pornography on the Internet. But what they don't realize is that such actions lead to bondage. You see, people tend to correlate freedom with the ability to do whatever they like. But this is not true freedom. Freedom has traditionally been understood as the power to do what one *ought* to do. That's why God's plan doesn't confine us, but actually sets us free! And this is precisely why Jesus said, "And you shall know the truth, and the truth shall make you *free*" (John 8:32).

4. People Benefit from Believing God Created Sex

The tragedy of the *Titanic* was caused by people who underestimated the danger of an iceberg. While the tip of an iceberg may seem harmless, the danger involves what cannot be detected by the human eye—the vast amount of ice hidden below the surface of the water. Likewise, our lives resemble an iceberg. People can see our actions and hear our words, but no one can see what lies below the surface—our beliefs. Yet it is our beliefs, more than anything else, that determine the course of our lives. It doesn't matter what we would like to believe, what people think we believe, or even what we say we believe. When crunch time comes, we make choices based upon what we *truly* believe.

This is why beliefs play such a central role in our successes and enjoyments in life. If you believe that you are likable, then you have a far greater chance of making friends. If you believe that you are smart, you are far more likely to succeed in school. And when it comes to relationships, people appear to benefit from the belief that God created sex. Just believing that God created sex for a purpose will benefit you in your future marriage! This is one strong reason why people who go to church are far more likely to have fulfilling sex lives than those who do not.

SOME FINAL ISSUES

Pornography

Pornography is destroying the very fabric of your generation. Few young people realize the devastating consequences connected with the viewing of pornography. With over 260 million pornographic Web sites on the Internet, sexual images are merely a click of the mouse away.[19] What was once only available to a few people willing to drive to a shady part of town can now be viewed by people of any age in the secrecy of their home.

Pornography can be defined as "the portrayal of sexually oriented material, in writing or in visual form, deliberately designed to stimulate sexually."[20] This includes videos, books, magazines, cable television, and the Internet. So why is pornography so dangerous?

- Brief exposure to pornography can lead to anti-social attitudes and behaviors.
- Pornography can diminish a person's sexual fulfillment.
- Viewing pornography often leads to increased fantasies about rape.
- Males who look at pornography easily become addicted and begin to desire more graphic or deviant material, ending up acting out what they have viewed.
- There is a demonstrated societal link between pornography and violence.

There are typically five stages people go through in the process of becoming addicted to pornography.[21] The first step is *exposure* to some type of pornographic material. The second stage is *addiction*. This step can take place only when a person chooses, as an act of the will, to travel down this path. During this phase people continually expose themselves to pornographic material because of a deep arousal and emotional satisfaction.

A third step is *escalation*. Because previous highs are hard to attain, users of pornography look for more explicit avenues to fulfillment. A fourth step is *desensitization*. Behavior that was formerly seen as shocking no longer seems taboo. Standards of decency and normality get set aside for the sake of more intense stimulation.

The final stage is *acting out* the fantasies. We do what we see. While every viewer of pornography will not become a serial rapist, many do look for new ways to live out their sexual fantasies. This is why Professor Robert Bork, former acting Attorney General of the United States, observed, "No one supposes that every addict of such material will act out his fantasies, but it is willfully blind to think that none will."[22] Remember, "Sow a thought, reap an act; sow an act, reap a habit; sow a habit, reap a character; sow a character, reap a destiny." This is why the apostle Paul says to take "every thought captive to the obedience of Christ" (2 Cor. 10:5).

If you are struggling with pornography, I *urge* you to talk with someone you know who cares. You are not alone. In fact, far more people struggle with pornography than you may realize. Please talk with someone—a youth pastor, parent, teacher, or friend—who will listen to you and help you.

Oral Sex

Not too long ago I had a discussion with a fifteen-year-old girl about her dating relationship. She was seeing an older boy and wanted some advice about how far she should proceed. After we had talked for about twenty minutes she casually made a statement that bewildered me. She said, "Well, we do have oral sex." What shocked me was not the fact that she was involved in this act (because this has been a growing trend in the past few years), but how casually she mentioned it. Sadly, what she didn't realize was that her decision to be involved in oral sex would have grave consequences for her future relationships.

Oral sex can be defined as the contact of one person's mouth with the genitals of another person.[23] Despite what many people might say, oral sex is just what we have named it—sex! It falls under the category of sexual immorality the Bible says to avoid outside of marriage. But oral sex has more consequences as well:

- Oral sex can serve as the route for transmission of *every* known STD, including HIV and HPV.[24]
- Oral sex is neither "safe" nor "safer" than traditional sex.
- Oral sex *before* marriage often brings emotional suffering *in* marriage. Oral sex can lock images into the mind that prevent someone from being truly intimate with his/her future spouse.

Oral sex is not simply an innocent act without consequences. There are physical as well as emotional consequences for being involved in it. *If any guy truly loved a girl he would never pressure her into oral sex, or into any sexual activity before marriage*. Any guy who says he loves a girl but pressures her into sexual activity is not telling the truth—period.

Standing Boldly for Purity

Abstinence is routinely dismissed as impossible for youth today because some say teenagers are "going to do it anyway." But such a perspective is insulting to teenagers. You are not an animal! In fact, teens are just as capable of controlling their sexual desires as they are controlling any other desire. I have heard it put this way: "You can live with the pain of your self control now, or with the pain of your choices later on." There is no other option. But let's face it, following a godly standard for purity *is* difficult today. There *are* a few things that a person can do to stand strong for sexual purity.

First, it is critical to avoid sexually tempting situations. Interestingly, the Bible tells believers to *resist* Satan, but to *flee* from sexual temptation.[25] This involves a choice—a deliberate decision—to avoid potentially compromising situations and to avoid sexually stimulating material. For example, it would be wise not to be in a house alone together, or, in fact, in anyplace without friends and supervision. The more things you can do in groups, the better off you will be. The Bible says not only to avoid evil, but to avoid even the *appearance* of evil.

GOD IS MORE CONCERNED ABOUT YOUR SEX LIFE THAN YOU ARE.

Second, it is important to have an accountability structure. Whether it is a parent, youth pastor, or friend, we all need someone who will ask us the following tough questions about our choices: Are you keeping your mind pure? Have you set sexual standards based on God's Word? Do you *truly* believe that God's plan for sex is best? Are you treating your boyfriend/girlfriend with dignity and respect? Is your relationship bringing you closer or further from God?

Third, ask God for help. One student said, "I asked God to help me control my passions and to show me how to have a relationship without sex. He helped me to avoid situations that were conducive to sexual response." It is important to remember that God is more concerned about your sex life than you are. If you provide the effort, God will provide the strength.

Forgiveness and Restoring Sexual Purity

Reading this chapter has probably been quite difficult for some of you. Maybe you feel like this young girl: "I had sex with my boyfriend, thinking I owed it to him. Later, when I learned I was pregnant, he blew up and said I should get an abortion—that it was all my fault. So, to save my parents heartache and to keep Matt, I had an abortion. Now Matt has left me. How can God love me after all I have done? I'm just so confused. Can God really love and forgive me?"

So often I hear young people say, "If you only knew what I had done you would know I can't be forgiven." My heart breaks when I hear this because I know it's so far from the truth. In fact, the truth is that *none* of us can stand totally pure before God. While some of us may have more painful issues to seek forgiveness for, we have *all* fallen short of God's perfect standard. This is the very reason that Jesus came to earth! After all, if we weren't sinners we wouldn't need a savior. "For all have sinned," as it says in Romans 3:23, "and fall short of the glory of God." But do not lose heart! There is good news, and it can be found in 1 John 1:9: "If we confess our sins, He is faithful and righteous to forgive us our sins and to cleanse us from all unrighteousness."

Although physical virginity cannot be restored, God can restore emotional and spiritual virginity. God can heal the emotional scars of past sexual experience and restore a person's hope for a fulfilling sexual relationship in marriage. One young woman put it this way in a letter to *Dear Abby*: "I was raped by a relative when I was a teenager. I spent the next five years searching desperately for love through numerous brief sexual encounters. I felt cheap and dirty and was convinced that no one could love or want me. Then I met a very special young man who convinced me that God loved me just the way I was, and that I was precious in his sight. I then let go of my burdensome past, and by accepting God's forgiveness, I started on the long road to forgiving myself. It works. Believe me. —*Free and Happy*"[26]

CONCLUSION

You are living in the most sex-saturated generation in history. Yet God calls you to a higher standard. God calls you to wait until marriage to have sex, not merely to steal your fun, but to protect and provide for you. And not only does God call you to abstain from sexual immorality, but he also calls you to a life of purity in thought and action. If you are willing to follow God's plan for sexuality now, you will have incredible fulfillment in your future relationships.

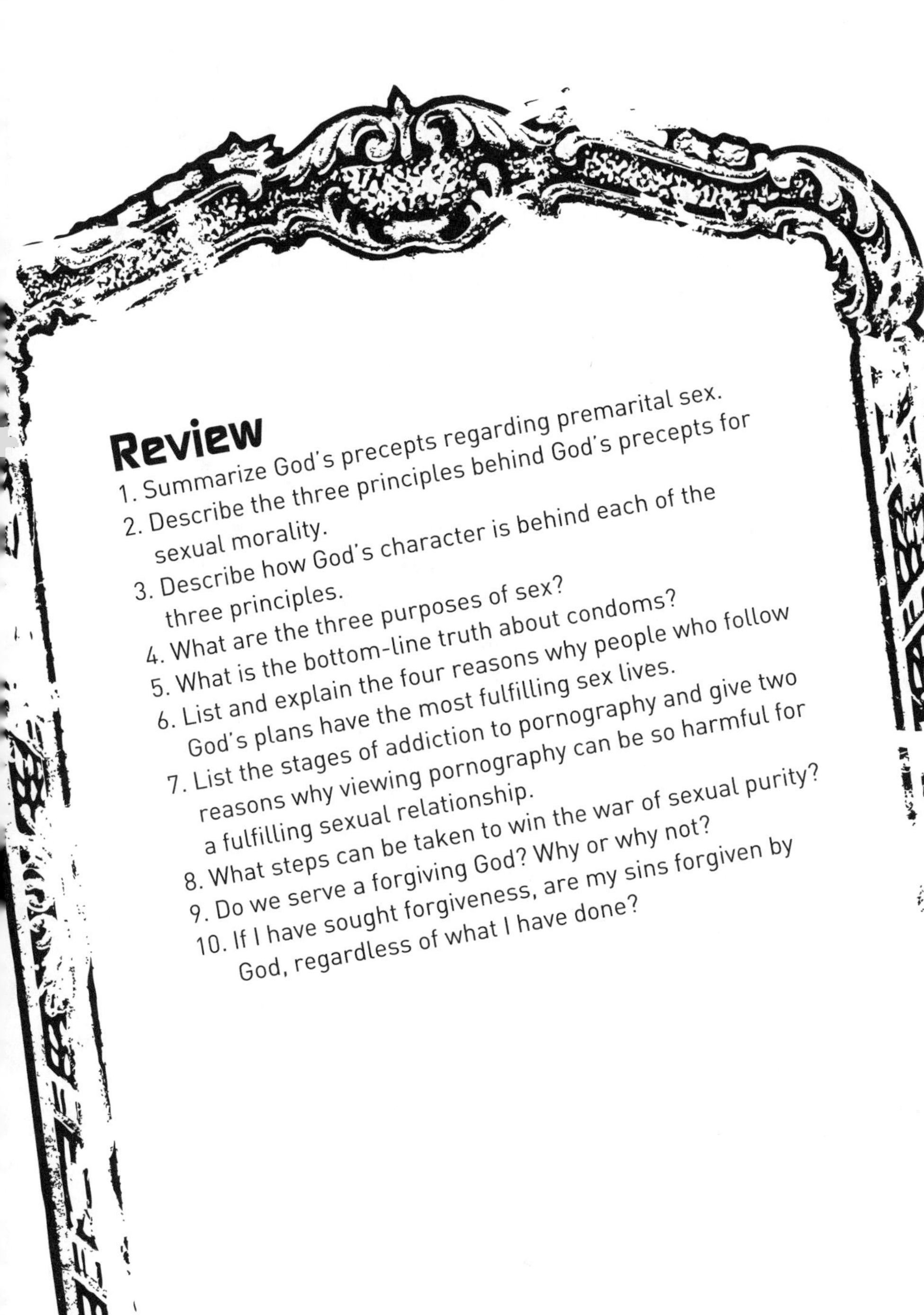

Review

1. Summarize God's precepts regarding premarital sex.
2. Describe the three principles behind God's precepts for sexual morality.
3. Describe how God's character is behind each of the three principles.
4. What are the three purposes of sex?
5. What is the bottom-line truth about condoms?
6. List and explain the four reasons why people who follow God's plans have the most fulfilling sex lives.
7. List the stages of addiction to pornography and give two reasons why viewing pornography can be so harmful for a fulfilling sexual relationship.
8. What steps can be taken to win the war of sexual purity?
9. Do we serve a forgiving God? Why or why not?
10. If I have sought forgiveness, are my sins forgiven by God, regardless of what I have done?

Small Group Discussion

1. Read the story of David and Bathsheba in 2 Samuel 11:1–12:14. As a group, list all of David's mistakes. At what point should David have stopped? The more David kept going the harder it was for him to stop. Have you found this to be true as well? After David's "fall," he immediately tried to cover it up. Have you ever tried to cover up a mistake? What was the result? Did David get away with his actions? What can we learn from his experience?
2. As a group, make a list of recent movies that deal with relationships and sexuality. Ask the following questions: How is sex portrayed in these movies? Are the consequences for premarital sex shown? Why do you think the media depicts such a false view of human sexuality? Specifically, how has the view of sex in the media affected you?
3. Consider again this statement: "Sow a thought, reap an act; sow an act, reap a habit; sow a habit, reap a character; sow a character, reap a destiny." Can a mere thought really shape your character, and ultimately determine your destiny? How does this relate to choices in the area of sexuality?

Drugs and Alcohol

PURPOSE

To consider the biblical and scientific data related to drug and alcohol abuse among young people today

In this chapter you will learn

- What the Bible has to say about drugs and alcohol
- Facts about the three most popular drugs among youth
- The purpose behind God's commands not to abuse drugs and alcohol
- Steps that can help you resist the pressures of drugs and alcohol

As a seventeen-year-old senior, Daniel wanted his prom night to be memorable. So on his way into the dance hall he reached into his jacket pocket and pulled out a couple of small pills imprinted with pictures of cartoon characters and popped them into his mouth. How harmful can a couple of pills from his friends be, he wondered? But Daniel learned the difficult way how dangerous drugs really are.

Trembling so badly from the drug, Daniel needed help from some of his friends to make it into the dance hall. But a few moments later Daniel hit the greatest high of his life. "Then I hit a peak," Daniel said. "I felt like a movie star!"[1] But later at a friend's house Daniel hit rock bottom. Even though this was the first time Daniel had ever taken ecstasy, he was immediately addicted. "I did drugs so I didn't have to feel alone," he said.

Soon Daniel was doing anything he could to feed his habit—stealing, lying, and eventually selling drugs himself. Finally, when his girlfriend called him a "lowlife" and a "drug addict," Daniel began to realize where his life was headed. "I got into drugs because I felt like no one liked me," Daniel said. "Then nobody wanted to be around me because of the drugs, and I ended up completely alone." In a search for happiness and fulfillment, Daniel found addiction, loneliness, and depression. Fortunately Daniel had the courage to seek help. Now Daniel is in a drug-rehab program getting his life turned around. When asked what he would say to other young people, Daniel responded, "I'd tell them, get out while you can. It starts out as all fun, games, and parties, but it leads to really nasty things. You become your own worst enemy."[2]

Many young people consider drugs one of the most common problems they face today. In most cases they turn to drugs in response to other problems in their lives. As a person who works with high school students every day, I am all too familiar with the stories of broken families, distant fathers, and emotional pain. My heart goes out to the young people who have to face difficult issues that God never intended for them to deal with. I can understand why so many young people turn to drugs—hoping to find momentary relief from the painful reality of their lives. But I also hear the stories, like that of Daniel, where lives are ruined by drugs. While I understand that many of you are seeking to feel better, I hope and trust you won't buy the lie that drugs will fill the emptiness in your heart. While drugs may offer temporary relief, they can no more fulfill you than a small adhesive bandage can fix a broken leg. As a matter of fact, they are dangerous and sometimes life-threatening. Only relationships with God and other people can truly offer your life meaning.

A BIBLICAL PERSPECTIVE ON DRUGS AND ALCOHOL

Spiderman is by far the coolest superhero! If you visit the classroom where I teach, you will see posters of Spiderman everywhere—my students have given me most of them. As a kid, I always dreamed about having a spider-sense. Just the thought of swinging from building to building in pursuit of Venom or the Green Goblin was enough to make my adrenalin run.

Growing up, I always looked forward to Wednesdays—the day the new Spiderman comic book arrived at the local grocery store. As soon as the school bell rang, I would run all the way into town to pick up a copy of the most recent issue of *The Amazing Spiderman* or *The Spectacular Spiderman*. As soon as I read it, I would store it away in a protective bag so it was safe from potentially damaging elements from the light or in the air. I was careful not to do anything to harm the quality of the comic book so as to negatively affect its value. Like baseball cards or stamps, even the slightest spoil on a comic can greatly decrease its value. Since I cared about each comic in my collection, I did everything I could to safeguard them.

One day one of my good friends asked to borrow a few of my Spiderman comics to read. I reluctantly agreed, trusting that he would not do anything to damage their condition. A few weeks later when he returned my comics, I found that he had violated the comic book collector's creed: *Thou shalt not do anything to hurt the value of a comic book.* He had bent the creases, pulled out a couple of staples, and torn a few of the pages. To say that I was upset is a great understatement. I couldn't believe that one of my best friends, who knew how much I cared about my comic collection, would take something I personally entrusted to him and treat it with such disrespect.

God also has entrusted us with something that does not belong to us—our bodies. Drug use and alcohol abuse, or partaking in any activity that negatively harms our bodies and causes addictions, is wrong for this very same reason. For us to misuse our bodies is to bring harm to something that is not our own. God gives us boundaries and guidelines regarding our bodies, not to ruin our fun, but for our safety and for his glory.

Our Bodies Belong to God

During the first century of the church, the people of Corinth were infamous for pushing the limits God had set for them to obey. In an attempt to get them back on track, the apostle Paul wrote the following in a letter addressed to the entire Corinthian church: "Or do you not know that your body is a temple of the Holy Spirit who is in you, whom you have from God, and that you are not your own? For you have been bought with a price: therefore glorify God in your body" (1 Cor. 6:19–20).

Once we become believers in Jesus Christ we willingly give possession of our bodies over to God. Bringing harm to our bodies destroys something that is not ours. Not only are drinking and smoking illegal for teenagers; they are wrong because they can so easily cause damage to something that is God's property and, I might add, his masterpiece!

In the passage above, Paul makes a comparison between the body of a Christian and the Jewish temple, which was first erected during the time of King Solomon. In Solomon's temple, God's presence was powerfully manifested so the Hebrews had a visible reminder that he was guiding them. Since God's Spirit was present in the temple, all who entered had to be absolutely spotless—no impurities were allowed. In fact, only the high priest could enter the most holy part of the temple once a year to offer a sacrifice to God on behalf of the people. If the priest was not fully clean in his dress or if he had any unconfessed sin, he was immediately struck dead. The temple had to be so clean because it housed the Spirit of God.

Since the time of Jesus' death and resurrection, the Holy Spirit no longer lives in the temple. The Holy Spirit has a new abode: "Do you not know that you are a temple of God and that the Spirit of God dwells in you? If any man destroys the temple of God, God will destroy him, for the temple of God is holy, and that is what you are" (1 Cor. 3:16–17). What does this mean for us? It means that we are called to be holy because God has chosen to make our bodies his home. Since the Spirit of the living God comes to live in our bodies, we must do everything we can to honor God's presence. Anything that brings harm to our bodies is destroying God's home.

Please understand this is *not theory*. This is fact—and one of the cornerstones of our faith that makes Christianity totally unique. How often do you think about the fact that the God of the universe lives inside you? This thought blows me away every time I think about it!

Love God with Our Minds

Jesus once was asked to name the greatest commandment from God. He responded by saying, "Love the Lord your God with all your heart, and with all your soul, and *with all your mind*, and with all your strength" (Mark 12:30). In other words, we are to love God with everything we have, including our minds. This means that we are not to be controlled by anything except the Holy Spirit. Anything that pollutes our minds, such as pornography or certain types of drugs and alcohol, prevents us from being able to love God in the way we are designed to. If our mental abilities are under the control of anything beside God's Spirit, we have forfeited God's power in our lives.

Like a computer virus, drug and alcohol abuse destroys the proper functioning of its host. Not too long ago I noticed that my computer was slower than normal and I couldn't log onto the Internet. Every time I tried to connect I received a signal that said, "Sorry, your connection attempt failed." One simple virus affected the proper functioning of my entire computer, and it took me weeks (and considerable expense) to find and solve the problem.

Drugs and drunkenness infect the mind in much the same way. When you give up control over your mind, you open yourself up for deception and manipulation. If you allow your mind to be controlled by them, then you forfeit your ability to function as you were designed to. In fact, you forfeit your freedom. Just as it is impossible to use a computer infected by a virus, it is impossible to live in the power of the Holy Spirit with a mind controlled by drugs or alcohol. Paul tells us that our minds are to be controlled by the Holy Spirit, not by external forces. It is only when your mind is controlled by the Holy Spirit that you will experience true freedom.

Drugs and Alcohol in the Bible

The Bible has quite a bit to say about the use and misuse of alcohol. Interestingly, it is not the use of alcohol that is wrong, but the *misuse*. In fact, in the proper circumstances alcohol is not always a bad thing. In his letter to younger Timothy, Paul encouraged him to take some wine for the benefit of his stomach (1 Tim. 5:23). In his very first miracle Jesus turned water into wine at a wedding in Galilee. Many scholars have noted that the wine in Jesus' day was much weaker than today's product. Yet the Bible is very clear that alcohol abuse is a grave sin that can have devastating consequences. It is often a seemingly innocent drink that opens up the door to later abuse. Scripture repeatedly calls drunkenness a sin (Gal. 5:21; Deut. 21:20–21). Proverbs 20:1 also warns of the dangers of drinking alcohol: "Wine is a mocker, strong drink a brawler, and whoever is intoxicated by it is not wise."

Many of the cultures that existed during the time of the Old and New Testaments were involved in sorcery and witchcraft. In the original language of the Bible, the word translated "witchcraft" is often *pharmakeia*, from which we get the English word "pharmacy." In ancient times drug use was involved in sorcery. It was impossible to separate the use of drugs from the practice of sorcery and witchcraft. This is why Paul strictly condemned such evil practices in Galatians 5:19–21.

While some people today use drugs merely to feel good, the occult link cannot be discounted. Interestingly, in an article in *Psychology Today*, one-fourth of marijuana users reported that they were controlled by an evil person or power during their drug trip. And over 50 percent reported experiencing religious or spiritual sensations regarding spiritual beings.[3] Although we may not fully understand it, there is a link between drugs and the occult that cannot be denied. Any follower of Jesus must steer as far from drugs as possible.

TYPES OF DRUGS

Alcohol

"Everybody I know drinks and drinks a lot." What surprised me when I heard this statement was not that it came from a well-known party-er at my school, but from a good student who is involved in leadership. Alcohol is clearly the choice drug among youth—and it is exactly that, a *drug.* While many people do not want to consider alcohol a drug, the scientific facts are incontrovertible. Alcohol impairs judgment and is highly addictive.

This is why King David got Uriah so drunk. You see, David had slept with Uriah's wife, Bathsheba, while Uriah was at war. Word came to David that Bathsheba was pregnant. Desperate to cover up his sin, David brought Uriah home to sleep with Bathsheba, hoping to absolve himself of his wrongdoing. But since Uriah refused to sleep with his wife while his country was still at war, David got him completely drunk and sent him home to be with his wife. The reason David got Uriah so drunk is that he realized a basic principle: *alcohol breaks down our ability to make sound judgments*. David thought that getting Uriah drunk would impair his judgment so he would make a choice that he would not make when sober. This is why in cases of rape, violence, and theft among youth, there is so often a link to alcohol. People simply do things when they are drunk they would not ordinarily do sober. When you are drunk you lose your freedom to think and act clearly.

Marijuana

Marijuana is made from the hemp plant that grows in many places of the world. Once a hidden drug, marijuana is now popularly used in our culture. There is much debate and misunderstanding over the effects of marijuana. Typically marijuana is smoked to create a relaxed feeling of ecstasy. But are there any negative effects of marijuana use? Let's look at these.

Ever heard the lame excuse, "But marijuana is a safe drug"? Tell this person to get the facts straight. Marijuana use often causes loss of coordination for athletes. But this is just *one* of the many side effects of the drug. You also might forget your best friend's phone number, watch your GPA drop like the temperature in a blizzard, or get into a car accident. Or even worse, consider a few of the more serious side effects of marijuana:[4]

- Marijuana use can lead to cancer or heart attack. In fact, smoke from marijuana has more agents that cause cancer than tobacco smoke.
- Marijuana damages brain cells and lung cells and often leads to infertility in men.
- Marijuana is considered by experts to be a "gateway drug" because it often leads to more dangerous drugs such as speed and cocaine.

Ecstasy

Ecstasy is considered a "club drug" because it is so often used at raves and all-night dance clubs. Rather than coming from a plant like marijuana, ecstasy is made from chemicals in laboratories hidden throughout the country. Makers often add various chemicals to ecstasy—such as caffeine and cocaine—causing the purity of the drug to be in question. Typically the pill is stamped with a comic image such as Tweety Bird or Mickey Mouse.

Like most other drugs, ecstasy appears to be highly addictive. Only fifteen minutes after taking the pill, ecstasy typically gives an initial "high," often causing the person to dance wildly for hours. The "hit" typically lasts between three and six hours. But like all other drugs, ecstasy has a substantial down side. After the initial high, the user experiences depression, loneliness, sadness, and anxiety. And besides this low point, ecstasy has many other dangers. Consider a few of the harmful effects:[5]

- Ecstasy can cause muscle tension, clenching of teeth, nausea, blurred vision, fainting, and chills or sweating.
- Ecstasy increases blood pressure and heart rate.
- Ecstasy can cause confusion, depression, sleep problems, intense fear, and anxiety.
- In high doses, ecstasy can lead to heart problems, seizures, liver and kidney failure, as well as muscular breakdown.
- Ecstasy has been linked to many deaths among teenagers.

THE PURPOSE OF GOD'S STANDARD

I will never forget a discussion I had with Dave, a co-worker at the 1996 Olympics in Atlanta. Working in a T-shirt stand gave me the opportunity to meet many unique people who had traveled from all around the world to see the Olympics. As an alcoholic, Dave constantly needed a beer or a glass of wine to make it through the day. While he knew I was a Christian, we had never talked about religion, God, or morals. In the middle of a discussion about sports he randomly spouted off these words to me with a bit of defiance: "You know, I am free to drink if I want to." I thought for a moment and replied by saying, "I agree that you are free to drink if you like. But I have another question for you. Are you free *not* to drink?" My point was simple: he was only free to drink if he could choose not to drink. But the truth is that he was a slave, a slave to his drinking problem. He had lost his freedom as soon as his behavior became an addiction.

Dave started drinking as a high school student. "What's the big deal?" he mused. "I am just having a couple of beers with my friends from class." He had no idea that what he considered to be an innocent activity with some friends would eventually destroy his family, career, and reputation. Just think about it for a moment. Do you think the teenager who went to a party with his friends to drink a beer for the first time *intended* to become the alcoholic father who is feared by his family and despised by his community? Do you think the football star who tried steroids so he could get a college scholarship *intended* to end his career because of the painful side effects? Do you think the pretty and popular cheerleader *purposefully* got hooked on drugs so she could end up in a drug rehabilitation program wishing she could end her life?

Of course not! Sadly, each of these young people had dreams and goals that were shattered by the very thing that they believed would bring temporary relief. I see young people making the same choices every day. This is why Proverbs 14:12 says, "There is a way which seems right to a man, but its end is the way of death."

You may be thinking, *It's no big deal. I just want to have a few beers with my friends. I won't get hooked.* But you need to realize that addiction *always* begins small. Many people have changed the course of their entire lives through mere experimentation. Truthfully speaking, *anyone* can get addicted. If you think it can't happen to you, then you are even more vulnerable because you are too proud to admit your weakness. To say that you are invincible is to mock God: "Do not be deceived, God is not mocked; for whatever a man sows, this he will also reap" (Gal. 6:7). It may be a struggle to resist, but God is with you and he will honor your choices.

HOW CAN I RESIST?

Resisting drugs and alcohol is not easy for many young people. We all want to fit in and be accepted. Not one of us wants to be left out. When it seems that "everyone drinks," it can become especially difficult to stand against the tide. It's also not easy because the media so endorses the idea that it is "cool" to drink. Television depicts a wonderful world where people drink, smoke, and have a great time without facing any of the real-life consequences. Beer commercials make it seem like a necessary factor, for fun is depicted as having a few beers to chug down with your buddies. Many students I know experiment with alcohol for the sheer thrill that comes from the experience. There seems to be something enthralling about doing something wrong and getting away with it. Many others drink simply to numb the pain in their lives—the pain of rejection, depression, and failure. So what can be done to resist such pressure?

A few years after contracting HIV, Magic Johnson created an audio series to help youth make responsible decisions in the area of sex. A student who listened to the series would be confronted with a series of questions that should be asked of anyone who was being considered as a sexual partner. They were questions such as, "Have you had sex with another male or female in the past six months?" or "Have you taken intravenous drugs?" While these would be important questions to ask any potential sexual partner, the reality is that teens often find themselves in compromising situations when it is too late to make such inquiries. That is why sexual standards must be set *before* one is in such a position. And the exact same thing is true when it comes to drugs and alcohol. NOW is the time to determine that you will live by God's standards. If you wait until you are being pressured, it is likely too late. Here are a few things you can do:

• ***Determine to have friends who will not lead you down a path toward addiction.*** You must make a conscious decision to stay clear of people who find amusement in things that are abusive and destructive. Find friends who believe as you do.

• ***Determine not to be in a potentially compromising situation.*** As a high school student I not only promised my parents I wouldn't drink, but I also promised I would not let anyone into my car who had even taken a sip of alcohol. I also refused to be at a party not chaperoned by a parent. Let me encourage you to make a similar pledge.

• ***Determine to seek help from people when you have problems rather than try to escape them or deal with them alone.*** One thing is inevitable in this life: you will face problems. You will have difficulties, and you will go through pain. Rather than trying to avoid problems, determine that you will confront them with the help of God and the help of others.

CONCLUSION

Drugs and alcohol are two of the greatest pressures youth feel today. While drugs promise a life of excitement and relief, the truth is that they lead to abandonment and pain. God does not ask us to avoid drugs to ruin our fun, but because he wants to set us free. God wants to spare us from the destruction that often results from experimentation with drugs and alcohol. God wants our lives to be clean so his Holy Spirit can indwell us with the power to live a meaningful and fulfilled life.

Review

1. Why is it important that our bodies are not our own?
2. Why does God not want our mental faculties to be controlled by drugs or alcohol?
3. What does the Bible have to say about the use of drugs and alcohol?
4. Explain some of the side effects for alcohol, marijuana, and ectacy.
5. Why does God give us a standard concerning drugs and alcohol?
6. How can drug and alcohol abuse be resisted?

Small Group Discussion

1. What do you think students are really searching for when they choose to become involved in drugs and alcohol? Is it simply for the thrill of the moment, or is it a deeper desire?
2. What creative ways can students have fun, create a sense of community, and enjoy each other without resorting to the use of alcohol and drugs? What can you do to reach out to the youth in your community who are searching for fun?
3. Read Proverbs 23:29–35. According to this passage, what happens to people when they allow alcohol to enter their lives?

Defending Pro-Life

PURPOSE

To understand the biblical, scientific, and philosophical foundations of the pro-life position and to be able to respond to common objections

In this chapter you will learn

- What the Bible has to say about the issue of abortion
- What the Scriptures say about the beginning of human life
- Philosophical issues related to the status of the unborn
- A three-step scientific case to defend the unborn
- How to respond to the most common objections in favor of abortionreality of truth against popular objections

Imagine you are a pregnant young woman with tuberculosis. The father of your unborn child is a short-tempered alcoholic with syphilis, a sexually transmitted disease. You have already had five kids. One is blind, another died young, and a third is deaf and unable to speak. The fourth has tuberculosis—the same disease you have. What would you do in this situation? Should you consider abortion? If you chose to have the abortion, you would have ended a valuable human being—regardless of the possible difficulties it may have brought you. Fortunately, the young woman who was really in this dilemma chose life. Otherwise we would never have heard the *Fifth Symphony* by Beethoven, for this young woman was his mother.

The issue of abortion is very personal to me. My youngest sister, Heather, was adopted into my family when she was just four weeks old. Even though I was only in fourth grade at the time, I will never forget the first time I held her as a newborn baby. Like all newborns, she weighed only a few pounds and was so precious and innocent. Now she is a beautiful young woman with an incredible heart for children. Her birth mother was a young, unmarried teenager, totally unprepared to support a newborn. While she could have chosen to have an abortion, our family is so thankful she did the right thing by choosing life. While her pregnancy may have been an inconvenience for her, the birth mother understood that even an unborn fetus is a valuable human being. It's difficult for my family to imagine what our lives would be like without the blessing of my sister Heather.

As you read through this chapter please keep one thing in mind: Abortion is not merely an academic issue—it involves *every* one of us. We all can be thankful that our parents were pro-life, because if they weren't, *none* of us would be here.

THE BIBLICAL BACKGROUND OF ABORTION

Although the Bible never explicitly says, "Abortion is murder," or "Thou shall not have an abortion," the tone of Scripture is unequivocally pro-life. The main reason Scripture does not directly address the issue of abortion is that abortion was so unimaginable to an Israelite woman it was not even necessary to mention it in the legal code. For one thing, children were considered a blessing from God (Ps. 127:3). Second, God is the sovereign ruler over conception in the womb (Gen. 29:33; 1 Sam. 1:19–20). And third, it was viewed as a curse to remain childless (Deut. 25:6). The Bible is silent about abortion because it was unthinkable in the Hebrew mind.[1]

Nevertheless, a powerful case against abortion can be made through understanding the principles of Scripture. Since the Bible clearly prohibits the taking of innocent life (Exod. 20:13), the key question in building a case against abortion is whether Scripture considers the unborn an innocent life, a human being made in the image of God. Does God value the lives of the born and unborn equally?

One helpful response to this question is to notice the language used in the Bible to describe the different stages of human development. Remarkably, the same words are used throughout the Old and New Testaments to describe the born and the unborn. For example, in the New Testament the Greek word *brephos* is often used of the unborn, newborn, and younger children (Luke 1:41, 44; 18:15; 1 Pet. 2:2), indicating that God views all stages of human development equally. And in the Old Testament the Hebrew word *geber* was used to refer to a person at conception but also to a grown man (Job 3:3; Exod. 10:11; Deut 22:5; Judg. 5:30). The popular distinction between the "potential life" of the fetus and the "actual life" of the newborn is found nowhere in Scripture. Every stage of human life has equal value in the eyes of God.

Conception as the Beginning of Human Life

The Bible repeatedly refers to conception as the beginning of a human being's history. Genesis 4:1 says, "Now the man had relations with his wife Eve, and she *conceived* and gave birth to Cain." In his misery Job cried out, "Let the day perish on which I was to be born, and the night which said, 'A boy is *conceived*'" (3:3). In his confession of murder and adultery, David traces his innate proclivity to sin back to his conception: "Behold, I was brought forth in iniquity, and in sin my mother *conceived* me" (Ps. 51:5).

God Relates Personally to the Unborn

Other passages describe God relating personally to the unborn. Job 31:15 says, "Did not He who made me in the womb make him, and the same one fashion us in the womb?" Psalm 139:13–14 states, "For You formed my inward parts; You wove me in my mother's womb. I will give thanks to You, for I am fearfully and wonderfully made; wonderful are Your works." And in Jeremiah 1:5, God says, "Before I formed you in the womb I knew you, and before you were born I consecrated you. I have appointed you a prophet to the nations." Here it seems evident that God had a personal relationship with Jeremiah in the womb as well as during his later prophetic ministry.

The Equality of the Unborn

Another biblical argument for the value of the unborn can be found in Exodus 21:22-23: "If men struggle with each other and strike a woman with child so that she gives birth prematurely, yet there is no injury, he shall surely be fined as the woman's husband may demand of him, and he shall pay as the judges decide. But if there is any further injury then you shall appoint as a penalty life for life."

This passage seems to indicate that if a woman gives birth prematurely yet the baby is unharmed then only a fine is appropriate. On the other hand, if the child (or the mother) dies then the offender must pay with his life. Killing an unborn baby carried the same penalty as killing a child who was born—even if the injury was accidental. This passage demonstrates a powerful point: if God requires such a harsh punishment for the *inadvertent* death of an unborn child, how much more harshly must he judge a *purposeful* abortion!

Some abortion advocates have contended the interpretation that the death of the baby results in a fine whereas the death of the mother requires the life of the offender. Therefore, it is often argued, the fetus is merely potential human life and is not deserving of the same level of legal rights as an adult person. This interpretation, however, has two core problems. First, the normal Hebrew word for "miscarriage" is not used here. Rather, the word for "premature birth" has connotations to live birth. The baby was not killed in this passage, just born prematurely. Therefore there is no precedent for considering the unborn baby to have less value than the mother. Second, even if this passage referred to a miscarriage, it is still not a sufficient defense for abortion because the injury was accidental, not intentional (as abortion is).

When God looks at the unborn he does not see a mass of tissue with the potential of becoming human. Rather, what is present at conception is considered equal to what is present at birth. A woman does not conceive a lump of cells, but a human person, a boy or girl. The Bible testifies to God's intimate care for the unborn.

THE SCIENTIFIC CASE

Many people mistakenly believe that abortion is merely a religious or philosophical issue. But this is false. The issue of abortion is primarily a scientific issue, and more specifically an issue of biology. What current scientific data has concluded is unmistakable: Conception marks the beginning of human life. In fact, prior to the *Roe vs. Wade* court case legalizing abortion in 1973, nearly every medical school book assumed or taught conception as the beginning of human life.[2] This fact is so well documented that no intellectually honest and informed scientist can deny it.

In recent years, technological innovations have allowed us to view the entire process of human development from the point of conception. The process can only be described accurately as miraculous![3]

- ***Conception:*** The beginning of life. Complete instructions for characteristics such as eye color, gender, height, and brain capacity are all contained in the DNA of the forty-six chromosomes inside the small cell. Even a trained geneticist cannot distinguish between the DNA of an embryo and an adult human being.
- ***Implantation:*** On day six, the individual burrows into the wall of the mother's uterus. The embryo's cells begin the process of dividing into the child's body and organ systems.
- ***Heartbeat:*** As early as the twenty-first day, the heart will begin to beat. The heart is beating rapidly by the third week and will continue to do so throughout the individual's life.
- ***Brain Waves:*** By the sixth week, the brain is forming basic functions. By this time the baby's body has already been developing and its fingers, lips, and mouth are perceptible.
- ***Organ Systems in Place:*** At week nine all body structures are present as the embryo becomes a fetus. The baby has fingerprints, eyelids, fingernails, and has the ability to grasp an object placed in its hand.
- ***Movement:*** At twelve weeks ultrasound allows parents to watch their baby moving around in the uterus—although the mother cannot feel the baby yet.
- ***Quickening:*** At about the sixteenth week, the baby is large and active enough for the mother to be aware of the baby's movement. At this stage the baby moves individual fingers, wiggles

his or her toes, and even makes a fist.

- ***Hearing:*** At twenty weeks the baby begins to respond to stimuli outside the womb. The baby is acutely aware of its mother's feelings of stress, pleasure, and excitement.
- ***Viability:*** As soon as twenty-three weeks, the baby can survive outside of the mother's womb. In rare cases babies have survived as early as nineteen or twenty weeks. At this stage the tiny baby can rest in the palm of an adult's hand.

The Three Steps of the Scientific Case

Not too long ago I visited a crisis pregnancy center. I took a tour of the facility while the director showed me the method their staff uses to convince virtually all pregnant women considering an abortion to give birth. Do you know what method they use that convinces nearly all women to keep their babies? It is the ultrasound. As soon as women are able to see a picture of the unborn baby inside them, they immediately realize that it is a precious unborn human being worthy of protection. But this is a conclusion not reached solely through observation; it also is widely supported by scientific data.

The scientific case for the pro-life position has three key steps.[4] The first *step involves showing that the unborn is alive*. Pro-choice defenders often express skepticism by saying, "No one knows when life begins." Despite the emotional appeal of this claim, it is simply false. Gregory Koukl observes, "The mother and father are alive. So are the individual sperm and egg. The zygote formed from their union is alive, as is the developing fetus during its entire term. Finally, the child delivered at birth is alive."[5] There is no stage in the process of development where the unborn is not living.

The second *stage of the pro-life argument is to show that the unborn is a separate individual from the mother*. Biologically speaking, it is a scientific fact that the mother and fetus are distinct individuals. Consider the following evidences:

- Many women carry babies with a different blood type than their own.
- A woman may be carrying a male child.
- The fetus has a DNA fingerprint distinct from the mother.
- If the embryo of black parents is transplanted into a white mother, she will still have a black baby.
- Early in development the fetus has its own hands, feet, heart, skin, and eyes.

The third *stage of the pro-life argument is to show that the individual is human*. A simple fact of life is helpful here: beings reproduce after their own kind. Greg Koukl explains this point. "A new being can only come from living parents and these parents reproduce according to their kind. Dogs beget dogs, lizards beget lizards, bacteria beget bacteria, etc."[6]

Therefore, if we want to know what type of being an offspring is, we ask a simple question: what type of parents did it have? Since beings reproduce according to their kind, something that is produced through the union of two humans must also be human. Therefore, at the moment of conception the unborn is a living, individual human being separate from the mother.

THE PHILOSOPHICAL CASE

When Does the Fetus Become Human?

Most people agree that the fetus either *already is* a human being from the point of conception or *becomes* a human being sometime during the process of gestation. Nearly all would agree that by the time the fetus is born, it is a human being with full human rights. Thus, the central question under debate is: when does the fetus become a human being? Various "decisive moments" have been suggested for when the fetus becomes fully human.

But before we consider the different "decisive moments," a preliminary issue must be discussed. Many suggest that no one can know for sure when life begins. It is often argued that the issue cannot be solved conclusively, so it should be left up to personal choice. In other words, since scientists and philosophers have not come to common agreement about the moment when life starts, it should be left up to the discretion of the individual.

While this may seem appealing initially, this approach is highly problematic, and here is why. Consider this example: if I were going to blow up a building but was unsure if there was anyone alive inside, should I proceed? Of course not. Ronald Reagan made this same point: "Anyone who doesn't feel sure whether we are talking about a second human life should clearly give life the benefit of the doubt. If you don't know whether a body is alive or dead, you would never bury it."[7] Therefore, even if there is uncertainty about when life begins we should err on the side of life. The benefit of the doubt goes to the life-saver. The burden of proof rests on the life-taker to show that there is no presence of life.

So, when do we become fully human? Abortion advocates have offered some "decisive moments" when this occurs.

Viability

Probably the decisive moment most commonly proposed is viability. *Viability* is the point at which a fetus can survive outside the womb with the commonly available technology. In other words, as soon as a fetus can survive apart from the nourishment and protection of the mother's womb, it becomes human.

One problem with viability is the difficulty of measuring it with any degree of accuracy. Fetuses vary in their ability to live outside the uterine environment, and, because of technological innovations, viability is getting pushed back, closer and closer to conception. Currently, viability begins around twenty-three weeks or earlier. But as technology improves, isn't it at least feasible that it could lower to twenty weeks, eighteen weeks, or even fifteen? In fact, with the development of the artificial uterus, why must there be a limit at all? As Dr. Scott Rae has observed, "Viability has more to do with the ability of medical technology to sustain life outside the womb than it has to do with the essence of the fetus."[8] Viability is not a sufficient measurement for the beginning of human life.

Brain Development

Another commonly proposed decisive moment is brain function, which occurs early in pregnancy. Since death is defined as the loss of brain activity, shouldn't the beginning of life be measured when the brain begins to function? This proposition has much appeal, but it is also problematic. For one thing, when a person dies, the brain condition is irreversible. But with the developing fetus the condition is only temporary. From the moment of conception the brain has complete capacity to develop, but, at death, that capacity is forever lost. Even if we granted that brain function determines the beginning of life, most abortions take place after the onset of brain functioning, so this criterion wouldn't justify the majority of abortions.

Sentience

Sentience is the moment at which a fetus can feel sensations, specifically pain. The allure of this proposal is that if the unborn cannot sense pain, then abortion is less cruel and therefore less problematic. Here's one reason to believe that sentience isn't what makes us human: this confuses the *feeling* of harm with the *reality* of harm. It is simply mistaken to necessarily associate the feeling of pain with the actuality of harm. For example, even if I could not feel pain in my legs from paralysis, I am still harmed if someone cuts off my leg. There are also many people who can't feel pain, but are nonetheless valuable. For example, those under general anesthetic, those in a reversible coma, and people suffering from leprosy often cannot feel pain, yet they are nonetheless valuable human beings. Our ability to feel pain is not what gives us value.

Quickening

The first time the mother feels the presence of the fetus inside the womb is known as *quickening*. For many years, especially before the dawn of advanced technology, it was believed that quickening indicated the beginning of human life. Quickening typically occurs at about four months into pregnancy. At this stage, the baby already has a heartbeat, basic brain functioning, every major organ, and has been moving for about seven or eight weeks.

The problem with this method for determining value can be answered with a few simple questions: How can the nature of the fetus be dependent on the mother's awareness of it? What if the mother was consistently drunk throughout the pregnancy and therefore never felt the movement of the fetus? Or what if the mother was numb? These questions reveal how ridiculous it is to determine the nature of the fetus by the physical sensations of the mother.

In light of the previous discussion, it is best to conclude that human life begins at conception. The argument could be stated in this way:[9]

1. Conception marks the beginning growth stage for an organism which ends in an adult human being.
2. There is no break in the process from conception to adulthood relevant to the essential nature of the fetus.
3. Therefore, from conception onward, the fetus is a human being.

Some have tried to challenge this argument by making a difference between "being human" and "being a person." The problem with this distinction is that it is completely arbitrary. Even the *Merriam-Webster's Collegiate Dictionary* defines a person as an "individual human."[10] Humanity and personhood necessarily go together—they cannot be separated. As John Ankerberg and John Weldon have observed, "Personhood and humanity do not grow; they are inherent. They are not something acquired; they are innate. No human being is 'more' human than another."[11]

Sadly, many people throughout history have used the arbitrary distinction between being a person and being human to disqualify certain people from their God-given rights. African Americans and Native Americans were once deemed "1/2 persons" or "3/4 persons" and treated inhumanely. In Nazi Germany the disabled were considered unworthy of life and killed to rid society of the "burden" of caring for them. Jews also were depersonalized in a similar way and then killed. In this same fashion, many people today depersonalize the unborn.

Scripture offers the only foundation for true human rights—that people are valuable *not* because of their skin color, intelligence, or physical appearance, but simply because they are humans made in the image of God. It is simply being human that makes one valuable. And the unborn, as we have seen, are *fully* human.

Important Differences between the Born and Unborn

While there is no difference between being a human and being a person, there are other differences between the unborn and a newborn. Pro-choice advocates often cite these differences as support for their position. While these are genuine differences, they are not significant enough to deny the valuable human nature of the fetus. The four ways are *size*, *level of development*, *environment*, and *degree of dependency*. SLED is a helpful tool to remember these differences.[12]

S – *Size:* The unborn are clearly smaller than newborns. But, does size have anything to do with the right to life? Is Shaquille O'Neal more human than Hillary Clinton because he is larger? Just because the fetus is smaller than adults does not mean it is not a valuable human person.[13] In Dr. Seuss's *Horton Hears a Who*, Horton says, "A person is a person no matter how small."

L – *Level of development:* The unborn are less developed than newborns and adults. But this difference has no relevance to its essential nature as a human being. Are adults more human than elementary school children because they have developed sexually? Are mentally handicapped people less human simply because they have not fully developed? The development of a human being begins at conception and continues throughout its entire life.

E – *Environment:* The unborn lives in a different location than the newborn—the mother's womb. But what does the fact that the fetus lives in the womb have to do with its being human? Do you stop being human when you change your location? How can *where* you are determine *what* you are?

D – *Degree of Dependency:* The unborn is 100 percent dependent upon its mother for survival. But why should this fact make it less human? If your humanity hinged upon how dependent you were, then what about toddlers, the handicapped, and those on dialysis machines? Are they still human? If we say the unborn are not human because of their dependence, then we deny those same rights to many other human beings outside the womb.

In light of this discussion, it is best to conclude that human life begins at conception. No point of time or moment exists between conception and birth when the fetus is anything but human. Therefore, the unborn deserves full human rights from the moment of conception.

ABORTION PROCEDURES

One of the primary reasons abortions are permitted in the United States is because few people are truly aware of the nature of the procedure. While there are many procedures used to kill the developing baby, the following are commonly used methods for different stages of pregnancy. Those who truly understand the procedure of abortion find it very difficult to support the practice. Many pro-abortion groups have worked hard to hide the details of abortion procedures from the public.

Partial-birth Abortion (Dilation and Extraction)

In this procedure the abortionist pulls the baby out of the birth canal by the legs. With the head still remaining inside, the abortionist crams scissors into the back of the baby's skull. The scissors are opened so that the brain can be suctioned out, allowing the abortionist to collapse the skull more easily. The baby is then removed from the woman and discarded.

Suction Aspiration

Typically when an abortion is done within the first twelve weeks, the baby is still small enough to be suctioned out of the womb. The suction apparatus used by abortionists—which is twenty-eight times as powerful as a household vacuum—literally tears apart the developing baby. The pieces of the baby's body are sucked into a container to be discarded.

Dilation and Curettage (D & C)

In this commonly used procedure, the abortionist inserts a knife into the womb to cut the baby into pieces. The baby has its arms, legs, and head cut off and its entire body shredded into small pieces. After the pieces are pulled through the birth canal they are carefully reassembled to ensure none have been left inside the mother that may cause future infection.

RESPONDING TO OBJECTIONS

"Women have the right to do what they want with their own bodies." There are two problems with this argument. First, the fetus is *not* part of the mother's body. As we have already seen, the fetus is a separate individual from the moment of conception. Second, it is *false* to say that a woman has the right to do whatever she likes with her body. No woman has the right to walk around without clothes, possess dangerous drugs, or hurt another person with her own body. A woman's right to her own body is not absolute—it is limited when it brings harm to another human being.

"If abortion becomes illegal, women will be forced into back alleys." This rejoinder can be answered with a simple question: Does society have the responsibility to make it safe to kill innocent people? If the unborn is a human being, as we have seen, then this argument has little force.

"Bringing these children into the world can be an economic drain." This rejoinder can be answered with a simple question: When humans become expensive, can we kill them? If this were true, should we then dispose of other people in society who are costly, such as the homeless? If the unborn is a human being, then cost is irrelevant to its right to life.

THERE IS NO STAGE IN THE PROCESS OF DEVELOPMENT WHERE THE UNBORN IS NOT LIVING.

"Women should not be forced to bring unwanted children into the world." This objection can be answered with a simple question: When people become unwanted, may we kill them? Dr. Scott Rae observes, "The fact that a child is unwanted is more of a commentary on the parents than the child, and if the fetus is a person, whether it is wanted or not is irrelevant to its right to life."[14]

"Women should not be forced to carry a baby resulting from rape." As emotionally devastating as it is for a woman to carry a baby under these conditions, this question is misleading because it avoids the real issue: Why should the child be punished for her father's crime? Should the law permit the murder of an innocent person to relieve the mental anguish of a trauma such as rape? While we need to show incredible love and understanding to a woman going through such a traumatic experience, we must not compromise on one key fact: *the unborn is a valuable human being*. The number of pregnancies resulting from rape or incest is very minute—roughly one in one hundred thousand cases. And furthermore, between 75 and 85 percent of rape victims who become pregnant choose to carry the baby to term.[15] Abortions from cases of rape are incredibly rare.

A POWERFUL ALTERNATIVE

Every year thousands of married couples are unable to have their own biological children. Desperate to have a child they can love and cherish, many couples decide to adopt. Sadly, there is a shortage of newborns available for adoption, which is why many couples have to wait years for their own opportunity. If you are faced with an unplanned pregnancy, or you know a young girl who is, please consider adoption. Not only will the life of a precious unborn human being be saved, but a family will be eternally blessed as well, as my family has been with the adoption of my sister Heather.

CONCLUSION

Approximately 1 million abortions are performed in America every year. Despite abortion's prevalence in our culture, the Bible, science, and philosophy all point toward the fetus being a fully valuable human being from the moment of conception. Ronald Reagan once summed up the importance of the abortion debate for our country: "We cannot survive as a free nation when some men decide that others are not fit to live and should be abandoned to abortion or infanticide. . . . There is no cause more important for preserving freedom than affirming the transcendent right to life of all human beings."

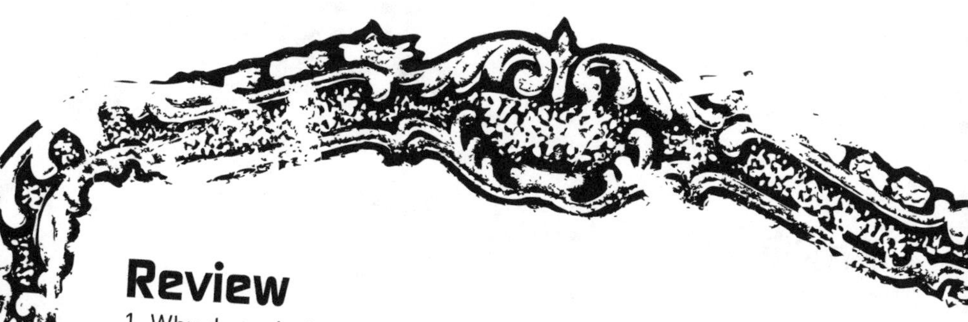

Review

1. Why doesn't the Bible directly address the issue of abortion?
2. How does Scripture support the pro-life position?
3. Explain why we should protect the unborn even if there was uncertainty about when life begins.
4. Explain why conception is the most logical "decisive moment" for the beginning of human life.
5. What are the four differences between the born and the unborn? Are these sufficient to deny full human rights to the unborn? Why or why not?
6. Give the three steps of the scientific case for pro-life with examples.
7. Respond to the following objections:
   - *Women have the freedom to do what they want with their own bodies.*
   - *If abortion becomes illegal, women will be forced into back alleys.*
   - *Bringing these children into the world can be an economic drain.*
   - *Women should not be forced to bring unwanted children into the world.*
   - *Women should not be forced to carry a baby resulting from rape.*
8. Adoption is a loving and courageous alternative to abortion. Why?

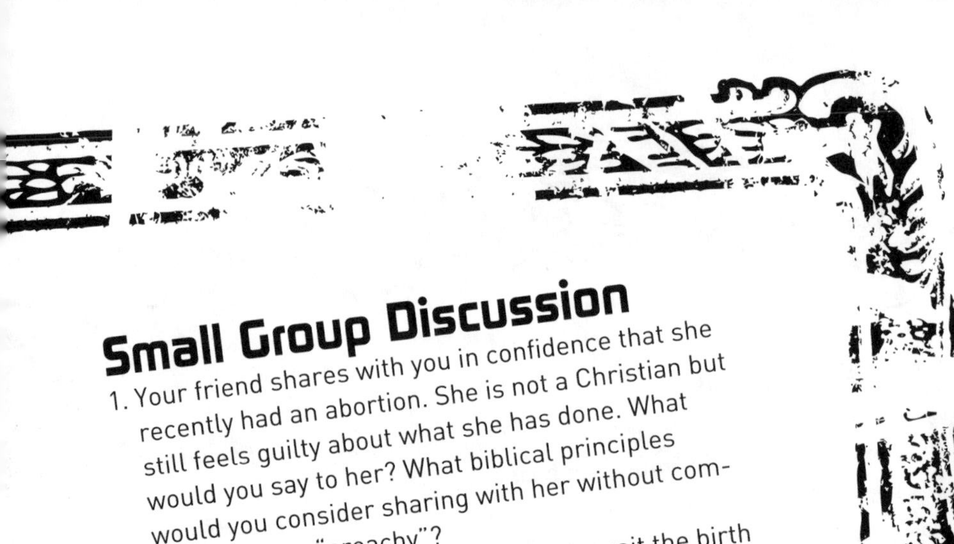

Small Group Discussion

1. Your friend shares with you in confidence that she recently had an abortion. She is not a Christian but still feels guilty about what she has done. What would you say to her? What biblical principles would you consider sharing with her without coming across as "preachy"?
2. David and Elizabeth Smith anxiously await the birth of their eighteen-week-old baby. During pregnancy their doctor informs them that the baby will have a birth disorder. Without pressuring them, the doctor mentions the possibility of abortion, which would allow them to start over with a healthy baby. Should Elizabeth have an abortion? Why or why not?
3. Patricia Watson, a nineteen-year-old college student at State University, recently became pregnant after being raped by a stranger. The trauma of the rape has been devastating for her. She wonders, "Why should I have to go through more pain in giving birth to this child who will be a constant reminder of my painful experience?" How could you respond to Patricia in both love and truth?
4. In what ways can you be *bold* and stand up for the unborn in your community?

Homosexuality

PURPOSE

To defend the Scriptural view of homosexuality using biblical as well as extra-biblical arguments

In this chapter you will learn

- The key difference between homosexual *attraction* and homosexual *behavior*
- What the Bible has to say about homosexual behavior
- The truth about the claim that homosexuality is biologically caused
- To consider extra-biblical arguments against homosexuality
- How we can respond in love and truth to those in the homosexual lifestyle

Imagine that, in your classroom, you are in an ethical dialogue, and you are representing the biblical perspective on homosexuality. Some of your classmates are known advocates for homosexuality, as is your teacher. Your classmates feel that homosexual relationships can be loving expressions of commitment. Any emphasis on "healing" a homosexual, they feel, is a waste of time, since they view homosexuality in the same way you view heterosexuality—as a gift from God. They argue that the Bible does not condemn homosexual acts, just perverse instances outside the context of love. You must defend, to your fellow students as well as to your teacher, the position that homosexuality is not a valid lifestyle. When it is your turn to speak, what will you say? What arguments will you use to explain your position?

Less than forty years ago, this class debate would have been unheard of. But beginning with the gay rights movement in 1969, proponents of homosexuality have made indelible inroads into virtually *all* aspects of American culture—including education, entertainment, and even the church. As a young person today you have no choice about the culture passed down to you. But you do have a choice as to how you will respond. Will you be *bold* enough to take a stand for biblical truth, even if it means being labeled an unloving bigot? Being able to take a stand for biblical truth is not always the easiest route. However, as we examine this issue, I want to challenge every reader to live by a higher standard.

THE BIBLICAL CASE

When asked why they disagree with homosexuality, most Christian young people reply, "Because the Bible says it's wrong!" While the Bible does condemn homosexual acts, few youth are prepared to respond to the evasive answers that many scholars give today to avoid the clear message in Scripture.

To fully understand why Scripture condemns homosexual acts, it is first necessary to understand God's original blueprint for human sexuality. In Genesis 1 and 2, God reveals that males and females were created in his image and likeness (1:27). After God made Adam, the Bible tells us that it was not good for man to be alone (2:18), so woman was created to fill Adam's relational need. God's original design for sexual relationships was for a man and woman to be together in the lifetime commitment of love and marriage. Sex within marriage is to provide pleasure, bring unity, and create new life.

Since homosexuality cannot fulfill the procreative and unitive dimensions of human sexuality as established by God, multiple passages in Scripture refer to it as unnatural. Homosexuality, as well as any other sexual act outside the confines of marriage, violates God's natural design for human sexuality.

Sodom and Gomorrah

In Genesis 19, Lot entertains two angels who came to the city to investigate the sins of Sodom and Gomorrah. At night all the men from Sodom surrounded Lot's house and demanded that he release his visitors so that they "may have relations with them." The men of Sodom did not know the visitors were angels, but they clearly desired to have homosexual relations with them. God harshly judged the sexual immorality of Sodom and Gomorrah by sending down fire and brimstone to completely destroy the cities. Though homosexuality was not the only element that contributed to their destruction, it was unquestionably a major factor.

Although there is a long history of both Jewish and Christian interpretations of this passage as referring to homosexual acts, more recently this traditional understanding has been challenged. Some revisionists have argued that the sin of Sodom and Gomorrah was not homosexuality but inhospitality. They argue that the visitors merely wanted to meet the guests and were anxious to extend Middle Eastern hospitality. It is often pointed out that the Hebrew word *yadha* that is translated as "have relations with," can also mean "get acquainted with." Indeed, throughout the Old Testament the word *yadha* appears more than nine hundred times, and only twelve times does it indicate sexual relations. Therefore, some people conclude, the sins of Sodom had nothing to do with homosexuality but inhospitality.

The problem with this argument is that it ignores the narrower context in which the story takes place—the book of Genesis. Of the twelve times the word *yadha* is used in Genesis, it refers to sexual acts at least ten times. Furthermore, the context makes it clear that the men were not interested in merely getting acquainted with the strangers. This is evidenced by Lot's reply: "Please, my brothers, do not act wickedly. Now behold, I have two [virgin] daughters who have not had relations with man; please let me bring them out to you, and do to them whatever you like; only do nothing to these men, inasmuch as they have come under the shelter of my roof" (19:7–8).

Lot's panic is evident as he rashly offers his *virgin* daughters to appease the angry mob—a sinful action in itself. This is not the action of a man responding to the crowd's efforts to "become acquainted with" the visitors. The fact that Lot refers to his daughters as "virgin" indicates he understood the demand from the crowd was *sexual*. Additional Scriptures also refer to the sins of Sodom as sexual.[1]

The Mosaic Law

The book of Leviticus records one of the clearest denunciations of homosexual practice in the Bible: "You shall not lie with a male as one lies with a female; it is an abomination. . . . If there is a man who lies with a male as those who lie with a woman, both of them have committed a detestable act; they shall surely be put to death" (18:22; 20:13).

The chief challenge to this passage is the claim that the laws found in Leviticus are no longer binding on believers today. For example, eating lobster and clam or planting different types of seeds in the same field were condemned in Leviticus. And since these prohibitions are no longer binding, critics argue, shouldn't the same apply to the laws against homosexuality?

To respond to this charge we must make an important distinction between two types of laws in the Old Testament: *ceremonial* laws and *moral* laws. Ceremonial laws were time-sensitive regulations so the Israelites could worship God and offer acceptable sacrifices to Him, such as the laws mentioned in the paragraph above. Moral laws, on the other hand, apply to the relationship between God and his people throughout all history. Simply because the prohibition against homosexuality occurs in Leviticus does not mean it was merely part of the ceremonial regulations. If this were true then bestiality, rape, and incest would be morally permissible, since they appear in the very same chapter as the prohibition against homosexuality.

John and Paul Feinberg observe: "As to the matter of the ceremonial versus the moral elements of the law, we can again agree that there are differences. The problem is that the distinction is irrelevant to the question of homosexuality. While there are ceremonial elements in the law that we may safely disregard today, most Christians as well as Jews have always recognized that there are commands within the law that are of continuing ethical significance."[2] The Leviticus passages that deal with homosexuality are part of God's moral law, and thus they are still binding on us today.

Moreover, even the Jews recognized a difference between punishment for breaking a ceremonial law by eating pork or lobster, which was a period of isolation, and that for homosexual acts, which was death. While Jesus did alter the dietary standard of the Old Testament,[3] the moral prohibitions against homosexuality are clearly repeated throughout the New Testament.[4]

THERE IS A DIFFERENCE BETWEEN HAVING A HOMOSEXUAL ATTRACTION AND ACTING ON IT.

The New Testament

The crucial New Testament text dealing with homosexuality is Romans 1:26-27: "Because of this, God gave them over to shameful lusts. Even their women exchanged natural relations for unnatural ones. In the same way the men also abandoned natural relations with women and were inflamed with lust for one another. Men committed indecent acts with other men, and received in themselves the due penalty for their perversion" (NIV).

Some have tried to interpret this passage as saying that homosexuality is wrong for those who are not *naturally* homosexual. This view claims that Paul is only condemning homosexual acts by heterosexual persons. Thus, if you are born heterosexual then heterosexuality is right for you. If you are born homosexual then homosexuality is right for you. To do otherwise is to violate your natural function. (This is similar to arguing that rape is morally permissible for the rapist who was born that way, but not the non-rapist.)

One of many problems with this position, as we will see, is that the evidence is lacking to support the view that homosexuality has a purely genetic cause. Even if such a cause existed, there is no reason to believe that Paul knew about it and refers to it here. Second, it is highly unlikely that when Paul says they "exchanged the natural function for that which is unnatural" he was referring to heterosexuals committing homosexual acts. As an educated Jew, Paul clearly knew that homosexual acts were against God's plan for sexuality as revealed in Scripture (Genesis 1–2) and as established in the order of nature.

It is striking that on *every occasion homosexual acts are mentioned in the Bible they are unequivocally condemned*. Because God is pure in his character, he detests acts of homosexuality. Make no mistake; the biblical testimony against homosexuality can only be neutralized by either radically misinterpreting the Scriptures or denying the authority of the Bible.

BUT I WAS BORN THIS WAY!

But isn't this unfair to the person with homosexual feelings? Heterosexuals at least have the chance of biblical marriage, but the person with homosexual longings has no such outlet. How can a person with homosexual inclinations be expected to remain chaste for his/her life?

Recent evidence indicates that a myriad of factors play a role in the development of sexual preference.[5] Genetics may give some push in the direction of homosexual liking, but as we will see below, it is not the *sole* cause. Disordered family relationships (such as a domineering mother and a passive or absent father) often leave young people deeply confused and unsure about their sexual identities. Early sexual experiences such as abuse or seduction also can play a role in the development of homosexual inclinations. Many young girls who were abused or deeply scarred by men turn to lesbianism. These young girls often view men as tyrants and lose the ability to trust or feel close to them. And research also has demonstrated a strong correlation between failed father-son relationships and homosexuality.

It is important to make a distinction between homosexual *attraction* and homosexual *behavior*. There is a difference between having a homosexual attraction and acting sexually, through either lust or deed, on that attraction. This truth is paralleled in heterosexual relationships. For example, it may not be a sin for a married man to be attracted to another person of the opposite sex. Yet that attraction becomes a sin when it is acted upon, either through lust or sexual activity. Similarly, homosexual attraction is not sin, but it becomes sin when it is acted upon. For instance, even Jesus was hungry after forty days in the desert, and might have wanted the food that the devil tempted him with; or, in his time in the garden before his crucifixion, he asked God to take the burden away from him, clearly showing his desire, but the fact that he acted well is what kept him pure.

It is important to note that the Bible doesn't seem to condemn homosexual attraction. God recognizes that our feelings, at least to some degree, may be beyond our control. But what does the existence of attractions or feelings have to do with God's *moral* call upon our lives? Because of our sinful human nature, we all are inclined to sin. Just because we ALL are born to sin—after all, every human being, once born, has sinned—does not make it acceptable to continue. Science has found that many other inclinations—such as alcoholism and propensity toward violence—also may be influenced by various factors. Is it unfair for God to expect sobriety and self-control as moral virtues? Of course not, because God has the right to call us to a higher standard. While people may not willingly choose their sexual attraction, it is their actions that God will hold them accountable for.

The Scientific Case

For many years scientists have been searching for a biological link to homosexuality. Finding such a cause would give credence to the commonly heard statement, "I was born this way." This would support the case that homosexuality is not a sin but a natural condition determined by our biological makeup. And if this is so, homosexuals would argue that they are entitled to full social and legal recognition. Three primary studies are cited for this biological link.

The Twin Study

Probably the most significant effort to advance the biological case for homosexuality was the study on twins done by Michael Bailey and Richard Pillard. They investigated homosexual men and their twin brothers, attempting to prove that sexual orientation is biological. In their study of male homosexuals they claimed that about 50 percent of identical twins were both gay. Pillard and Bailey concluded that genetics account for the high percentage of homosexuality among identical twins.

There are several concerns that need to be raised about this study. Two will be briefly mentioned here. For one thing, other recent studies have produced radically different results.[6] The second problem is this: If genetics are determinative, why are nearly half of the identical twins *not* homosexual? If sexual orientation was determined completely by genetics then *all* twins should be 100 percent equally homosexual. But this simply isn't the case. Even Bailey recognized that "there must be something in the environment to yield the discordant twins."[7]

The Brain Study

Dr. Simon LeVay studied the hypothalamus region of the brain to determine if there was a difference in size between heterosexual and homosexual men. In studying forty-one cadavers, he found that some of the neurons in homosexual men were smaller than those he found in heterosexual men. He argued that this size variation accounts for sexual orientation.

Several problems have been cited with this study. First, LeVay has since admitted that his findings were distorted and overstated in the media.[8] Second, no scientist has ever demonstrated a link between the area of the hypothalamus under discussion and a cause for sexual orientation. No one really knows conclusively if this area is even *related* to sexuality.

Another problem for LeVay's brain study is that the sexuality of the subjects was questionable. LeVay assumed that some of the subjects were heterosexual because there was no official mention of sexual orientation in their medical charts. But the fact that many of the heterosexual subjects died of AIDS makes their heterosexual orientation highly suspicious. And finally, corroborating studies to support LeVay's findings are lacking.[9]

The Genetic Study

In 1993, Dr. Dean Hamer claimed to have found a genetic link to sexual orientation. The media heralded his study as the discovery of the "sexual orientation gene." In an examination of seventy-six men recruited from an AIDS treatment program who met the criterion of having a gay brother, Hamer's team found a strong pattern of homosexuality in maternal relatives over and above paternal relatives. This suggested that homosexual orientation might be inherited through the X chromosome of women.

Though this study was heralded in the popular press as evidence for the "gay gene," there are significant concerns that must be raised about the findings. First, we still have the problem of cause and effect. Just because a majority of the homosexual men have shared genetic variations does not mean this variation is the cause of their homosexual orientation. And what about the minority who were homosexual but did not have the genetic variations?

Second, these findings have not been replicated by other research teams. One newspaper even reported a failed attempt at replication of his studies in a Canadian laboratory.[10] This same newspaper article has raised serious allegations of scientific misconduct against a particular researcher on the Hamer team. Psychologists Stanton Jones and Mark Yarhouse summarize the significance of the claims by Hamer et al.: "The major limitation of these studies is that they did not, contrary to the media reports about the first study, find a sexual orientation gene. They rather appear to have found a cluster of shared genetic segments which seem to relate to sexual orientation in this unusual and selective sample of homosexuals. . . . It is quite clear that these studies did not find a chromosome which causes homosexual orientation."[11]

The chief reason science will *never* show a full physical cause for homosexuality is because sexual preference is not solely physical—it's at least partially developmental. One could make a comprehensive physical examination of one thousand people—their genes, sex organs, hormone levels, etc.—and never determine *solely from the physical evidence* which of them prefer the same sex. In fact, we wouldn't even be able to know *any* particulars about their sexual tastes (do they like blonds or redheads?) by examining their physical makeup.

But even if science did show a genetic cause for homosexuality, would that justify homosexual behavior? The simple answer is this:

just because a behavior is natural does not mean it is right. Think about it for a moment. Does a natural propensity toward violence justify mugging someone? Does a natural desire for food justify stealing it? While animals do what comes naturally to them, human beings are moral and rational creatures that can rise above their natural appetites and act in the best interest of society.

Sometimes abiding by our natural instincts can be perilous. The "natural" reaction of a child whose clothes catch on fire is to run as fast as possible to try to escape the flames. But the wise response is to ignore our natural inclinations and to stop, drop, and roll. Even if science could show that homosexual feelings were natural, it would still not justify the homosexual behavior.[12]

EXTRA-BIBLICAL ARGUMENTS

Making a persuasive case against homosexuality without examining the Bible is a challenging task. But with an understanding of moral and philosophical considerations it can be done. Below are the three primary arguments against homosexuality from a non-biblical perspective.

The Danger of Homosexual Practice

A popular argument against homosexuality is the link between homosexual practice and AIDS. There is no question that homosexuality has been one of the key methods of transmission of this deadly disease (as well as many other STDs). It also has been spread by homosexuals to hemophiliacs through blood transfusions, wives of bisexuals, users of shared needles, and others. Thousands of lives have been lost as a direct result of homosexual practice. Any civil society would condemn such a dangerous act to protect the health of its citizens.

While this is a powerful point against homosexual practice, the fact of the matter is that AIDS has also spread quickly among the heterosexual community (although with far less prevalence than in the gay community). But this brings us to the core problem of homosexual behavior: its *inherent* danger. Even protected homosexual relations are dangerous because of the implications for the human body. While heterosexual behavior is dangerous when taken out of its original design, homosexual behavior is dangerous in *any* context. It cannot be made safe. While some of the non-safe elements can be minimized, homosexual behavior itself is a danger to society. Consider a few of the following health concerns linked to homosexual behavior:[13]

- Researchers report a significantly higher rate of drug and alcohol abuse among homosexuals.
- Certain mental disorders occur at a much higher rate among male homosexuals.
- Male homosexuals have a 75 percent lifetime STD incidence rate.
- Physical trauma to the body is a common problem because of the nature of certain homosexual acts.

Homosexuality Is Not Natural

Proponents of homosexual rights often argue that homosexuality is natural, especially since it can sometimes be observed in the animal kingdom. On the surface, there seems to be some truth to the claim that homosexuality is natural. But a deeper analysis reveals serious flaws in using this to justify human homosexuality.

There is a basic difference between male homosexuality and homosexual acts in the animal kingdom.[14] Males commit homosexual acts not just because they are erotic, but because they are *male* erotic. They are not merely attracted to a physical body part, but to their own gender. Animals, on the other hand, merely desire to be stimulated. They are not attracted to the gender of the animal, which is why a dog will mount a sofa, a tree, or even your leg. While this example may prove that animals masturbate, there is no evidence that their homosexual desires parallel the desires of humans.

But even if the relevant homosexual acts did occur in nature, would we want to use that as justification for human homosexuality? If we accept this type of reasoning then we also would have to justify cannibalism and murder. Why? A good example can be found in the life of the black widow spider. After mating, the female black widow kills her mate and then eats his body. To be consistent, we also would have to justify these abhorrent actions that occur in nature as well. And except for a few radical feminists, I can't think of too many people who would want to justify that!

But there is another sense in which "natural" is used, mainly to refer to events that "occur in nature." As before, however, the same problem arises because all sorts of wild things occur in nature—rainforests being depleted, babies drowning, incest, and even homosexuals being bashed for their beliefs. All of these would be considered natural because they "occur in nature." And, by this definition, humans are part of nature, and therefore human conduct would be natural. Practically everything would have to be considered natural by this definition.

DESPITE THEIR SINFUL BEHAVIOR, HOMOSEXUALS ARE WORTHY OF GRACE, LOVE, AND COMPASSION.

But generally people mean something different when they refer to things occurring in nature. Greg Koukl explains, "Things are natural if they fit the pre-technological, natural order of things; they are functioning according to their primitive *pattern* or *purpose*."[15] Therefore, a natural sexual desire is one that fits the original pattern or purpose of sexuality. And the natural purpose of sex is reproduction, passing one's genes on to offspring. But since homosexuals can't reproduce according to this pattern, this definition of "natural" can't be used to defend homosexual behavior either.

Additionally, wouldn't one consider it unnatural if someone had a nose but couldn't smell, eyes, but couldn't see? Then why is it considered natural for someone to have the male sex organs but be dispositionally incapable of using them for their reproductive purpose with the opposite sex? Homosexual behavior is simply not a natural use of the human body.

No Society Can Survive by Homosexual Practice

Human culture depends for its very existence on healthy heterosexual relationships. Apart from healthy heterosexual relationships there could not even be homosexual relationships. Simply put, no one was ever born of a homosexual union. Heterosexual relationships are absolutely necessary for the preservation of the human race, and, without them, humans would be extinct within one generation. In the aforementioned sense, homosexuality is a threat to the continuance of the human race. It would not be sufficient to argue that this will not happen, since only a small percentage of the population is gay; if society deems it an acceptable practice, then all could theoretically practice it. And then, of course, if everyone did practice it, the human race would self-destruct.

RESPONDING TO OBJECTIONS

"People should have the freedom to express themselves sexually without constraints." Let's imagine for a moment that this is true—people *should* have the freedom to express themselves without sexual restraints. Does this apply to the adult man who desires to have sex with young boys? If this is how he wants to express himself, would that make it right? This behavior is wrong regardless of his desires. Clearly there are restraints we set on sexual behavior.

"Homosexual acts are fine as long as no one gets hurt." The problem with this claim is that it is simply naïve. Homosexual behavior does hurt people. Sin is so powerful that someone *always* gets hurt, even if it is solely the perpetrator. In fact, recent studies indicate that homosexual men are four times as likely to be alcoholics as heterosexual men and six times as likely to commit suicide.[16] Homosexual behavior does hurt people. Many parents have been hurt because their gay children will never produce grandchildren. But even if no one gets hurt, homosexual behavior is still wrong. It is not in the consequences of one's actions that right and wrong are found, but in the deed itself. Many actions—such as lust or lying—are wrong in themselves, even if no one gets hurt. It is that one is disobeying God. Some people are hurt even by doing the right thing, are they not?

"But homosexuals have made such wonderful contributions to society." Of course, in many instances this is true—homosexuals have written great literature, been great war heroes, composed beautiful music, and contributed in many ways to the benefit of our society.

But, we must ask, what does this have to do with the morality of their sex lives? They did these great things as human beings, not because of their sexual preference. Elton John, for example, is a great musician. He has also admitted to being a homosexual. What is the relationship between the two? There is none.

"You may think homosexuality is wrong, but you have no right to force your views on others." Actually, the issue of forcing one's morality on another is debatable. In fact, every law in existence forces someone's view on another—that's the nature of the law. Our government forces its morality on rapists, thieves, and other lawbreakers all the time. But the point is not about who is forcing a version of morality on another. The point is that many homosexuals want full approval for their lifestyle and they want to silence your ability to object. Next time someone gives you this line you may say, "You may think homosexuality is acceptable, but what right do you have to force your view on me?"

HOW SHOULD WE RESPOND?

Homosexual people are very much like us—they want love, forgiveness, friendship, and acceptance. Many feel abandoned by the world, and sadly, many feel (and some are) rejected by the church. So as Christians, we have an important role to play. We must not compromise the clear biblical teaching that homosexuality is immoral; but, not to be forgotten is that, in our relationships with people, we need to stand firm on the biblical truth that all people, despite their sinful behavior, are made in God's image, and therefore worthy of grace, love, and compassion.

Demonstrating the Love of Jesus

When asked what I *think* about homosexuals, I often reply, "I think homosexuals, like all people, are made in the image of God. They are worthy of respect and should not be bashed or made fun of because of their sexual preference." And this is true regardless of how immoral their behavior might be. No human being is a fag, a scumbag, or a piece of dirt. As Christians, we ought never talk or joke about homosexuals in such a way that insults or hurts them. It always breaks my heart to see Christians hold up signs at rallies that say, "God hates gays," or "Fags are going to hell." I can't imagine Jesus or the disciples treating a human being with such indecency.

At the 1996 Olympics in Atlanta, I met a middle-aged man I will never forget. While selling T-shirts inside Centennial Park, a man covered with rainbow flags approached my booth. I asked him what country his flags were from and he responded bluntly, "Oh, they're just a queer thing. You see, I'm gay." So I replied, "Do a lot of people make fun of you for being gay?" Instantly he said, "Yes, I hear demeaning statements all the time." I looked him directly in the eyes and said these words with the utmost sincerity: "I'm really sorry that people treat you that way. It's not right." Behind his eyes was a hurting and broken man. He thanked me over and over again, and in fact he asked me if he could take his picture with me because he said I was the nicest person he had met at the entire Olympics.

What I have done is just make a distinction between my attitudes about homosexual *people* and my conviction concerning homosexual *behavior*. If we begin a conversation by saying, "I think homosexuality is immoral," we will be accused of hate speech and people will not hear our reasons. But if we demonstrate understanding and respect, then we just might earn the right to be heard.

Speaking the Truth

If we truly love, we will not be afraid to speak God's view of homosexuality or any other issue. In a world that tells us not to judge and to be tolerant of *all* views, God calls us to the higher standard of truth. Don't be deceived: these days, more and more Christians are regarded as unloving on the basis of viewing homosexual behavior as wrong. Be ready, if you are bold enough to speak the truth, to be called names such as *bigot, intolerant,* and *judgmental*. Even so, aim to be genuinely loving when you do speak. As the apostle Peter said, "But in your hearts set apart Christ as Lord. Always be prepared to give an answer to everyone who asks you to give the reason for the hope that you have. But do this with *gentleness* and *respect*" (1 Pet. 3:15 NIV).

CONCLUSION

Both the Old Testament and the New Testament teach heterosexuality as the basis of God's design for sex. Any other sexual activity—whether premarital sex or homosexuality—is outside God's design, and is therefore wrong. This is not only demonstrated in Scripture, but also through a scientific analysis of the natural world. But, if we are truly going to follow the example of Jesus, we must *never* forget to demonstrate God's love just as powerfully as we teach the truth.

SCRIPTURE REFERENCES TO HOMOSEXUALITY

- Genesis 19
- Leviticus 18:22; 20:13
- Deuteronomy 23:17–18
- Judges 19:22–30
- 1 Kings 14:24; 15:12
- Ezekiel 16:50
- Romans 1:26–27
- 1 Corinthians 6:9
- 1 Timothy 1:10
- 2 Peter 2:7–10

Review

1. Describe God's original blueprint for human sexuality.
2. Respond to the revisionist claim that the sin of Sodom was inhospitality.
3. Respond to the charge that the prohibition of homosexuality in Leviticus no longer applies to today.
4. State and defend the critical New Testament text against homosexuality.
5. Why are some scientists so eager to find a biological link to homosexuality?
6. Give at least two problems for each of the studies mentioned below.
   - The Brain Study
   - The Twin Study
   - The Genetic Study
7. Describe the three extra-biblical arguments against homosexuality.
8. How can we respond to the gay movement in both *love* and *truth*?

Small Group Discussion

1. Brainstorm together to think of additional justifications used by people to support homosexual behavior. Then see if you can come up with an appropriate reply to each of the challenges.
2. How can we make the church of the next generation one in which people who struggle with unwanted homosexuality feel supported, understood, and welcome in the church?
3. How has the media over the past few years contributed to the greater societal acceptance of homosexual behavior?

The Case for Marriage

PURPOSE

To understand God's design for marriage and to consider the challenges brought by divorce and same-sex unions

In this chapter you will learn

- To understand the four primary purposes of marriage
- The truth about divorce and remarriage
- Why healthy marriages are so important for the well-being of society
- Why marriage must not be redefined to include same-sex unions

In the 1993 comedy *Mrs. Doubtfire*, Robin Williams plays a creative writer and producer estranged from his kids because of his painful divorce. At one point when Williams is discussing visitation rights with his ex-wife he says, "You ripped my heart out. Did you come back to do it again?" Because a judge ruled that he could see his kids only once a week, Williams goes into a depression. Desperate to spend time with his kids, he applies for the position of his ex-wife's housekeeper. With a grandma's wig, a little makeup, and the perfect dress, he becomes Mrs. Doubtfire, a devoted British housekeeper who gets hired on the spot.

Although the movie is very well written and quite funny, it has a subtle agenda. In the final scene of the movie, Mrs. Doubtfire gives a brief speech, illustrating this agenda. She exemplifies a common belief about marriage and divorce in our culture: "Some parents when they are angry get along much better when they don't live together. They don't fight all the time and they can become much better people—much better mommies and daddies." In an attempt to avoid children of divorce feeling bad, the movie ends up speaking half-truths. No doubt divorce may be the best for the kids when abuse or cheating destroys the fabric of a marriage. But is it really true that divorce is *often* the best option when mom and dad simply have relational problems that are difficult to reconcile? While the intention of the movie is noble, do people typically become better parents when they divorce?

Until recently, divorce was a somewhat rare phenomenon. Yet today nearly one in two marriages ends that way. As Andrew Schepard, one of the country's leading divorce researchers, said recently, "Americans have come to view divorce as a natural experience."[1] There was once a stigma attached to divorce, but now it is considered not only an ordinary aspect of life, but often times even the *best* option. Sadly, some couples today pledge to keep wedding vows, "So long as they both shall *love*."

Yet divorce is not the only issue facing the institution of marriage today. Many people want to reinvent the notion of marriage to include same-sex unions. In fact, many foreign countries, such as Canada, have changed their definition of marriage to include such unions. "As long as people love each other," it is argued, "why shouldn't they be allowed to marry? Why should society defend traditional marriage from same-sex unions?" Should marriage be redefined to include same-sex unions?

There are few issues more important for the health of society than the issue of marriage. What is the purpose of marriage? And why is marriage so important? As a young man or woman, it is critical that you understand the biblical as well as societal role of marriage. Understanding the importance of marriage will help you not only to have a successful marriage in the future, but also to take a stand in our society that so often belittles the sanctity of marriage.

THE PURPOSE OF MARRIAGE

The best way to understand the purpose of marriage is to consider the creation account in Genesis 2. Genesis 2:18–24 reveals that marriage is God's, not man's, idea. After creating the world and man, God decided it was not good for man to be alone. Adam systematically named all the animals, but none of them was a suitable helper. So God made Eve from Adam's side. I can only imagine what Adam was thinking when he first saw Eve, the pinnacle of God's creation! The marriage passage ends with the following command: "For this reason a man shall leave his father and his mother, and be joined to his wife; and they shall become one flesh" (2:24). A few implications for marriage emerge from this account.

Marriage Is between a Man and a Woman

Biblically, a marriage must be between a male and female. This is very clear from Genesis 1:27–28, where God created "male and female" and commanded them to "be fruitful and multiply, and fill the earth." Reproduction can take place naturally only through the union of a male and female. Paul further states that marriage is between one man and one woman: "each man is to have his own wife, and each woman is to have her own husband" (1 Cor. 7:2). Even Webster's dictionary defines *marriage* as "The mutual relation of husband

and wife."[2] God did not create two men, two women, or any other variation. Marriage is between one man and one woman.

Marriage Is about Wholeness

The only thing that was not "good" about creation was the fact that man was alone. Man is incomplete by himself—he needs a mate. One of God's primary purposes for marriage is that a husband and wife experience loving fellowship and oneness. God's desire is that they are, in marriage, unified in both body and spirit. Marriage is the proper context for sexual union, but it is also a companionship that goes far beyond sexuality (Mal. 2:14). It is a partnership that includes sharing of interests, activities, purposes, and dreams.

Marriage Is about Kids

The first command in the Bible is for men and women to multiply and fill the earth (Gen. 1:28). This is one command of God that mankind has taken seriously! What makes human procreation different from that of animals is that it is to occur in the family context, according to God's pattern. Scripture is clear that mom and dad are to raise their kids in a godly home. While not all married couples choose to have kids, marriage is intrinsically about and for children (Mal. 2:15).

Marriage Is a Lifelong Commitment

The Bible is very clear that marriage is permanent in this life. This is what Jesus referred to when he said, "So they are no longer two, but one flesh. What therefore God has joined together, let no man separate" (Matt. 19:6). Paul also makes this clear in Romans 7:2, "For the married woman is bound by law to her husband while he is living; but if her husband dies, she is released from the law concerning the husband." Although marriage is a lifelong commitment, it is not eternal. While we will surely be able to recognize our loved ones in heaven, Jesus made it clear that we will not maintain our marriage in the afterlife (see Matt. 22:23–30).

DIVORCE

The Biblical Facts about Divorce

The Bible makes it clear that divorce is not God's ideal. In fact, God said to the prophet Malachi, "I hate divorce" (2:16). While God sometimes permits divorce, he never intends it. This is made clear in Matthew 19:8. After answering questions from the Pharisees regarding marriage and divorce, Jesus says in private to his disciples, "Because of your hardness of heart, Moses permitted you to divorce your wives; but from the beginning it has not been this way. And I say to you, whoever divorces his wife, *except for immorality*, and marries another woman commits adultery."

In the preceding passage Jesus gives one criterion for permissible divorce—immorality. But what exactly did Jesus mean by immorality? *Porneia* is the word from the original biblical language which is translated as "immorality." While there is much debate about the meaning of porneia, it seems to be best understood as referring to acts of sexual impurity such as adultery, homosexuality, and incest.[3] Jesus is saying that anyone who divorces a spouse for any reason besides sexual immorality is, in God's eyes, still married. Therefore, to divorce and remarry, except in cases of porneia, is to commit adultery.

Paul gives two more exceptions where the marriage bond is dissolved and remarriage is permissible. The first occurs at the death of one of the partners (see Rom. 7:3). The second condition is when an unbeliever is married to a believer and the unbeliever chooses a divorce. Paul says, "Yet if the unbelieving one leaves, let him leave; the brother or the sister is not under bondage" (1 Cor. 7:15). If an unbeliever deserts a believer, then the remaining faithful partner is freed from the bonds of the marriage. No other exceptions for justifiable divorce are explicitly mentioned in the Bible. Nevertheless, many argue that divorce is justified in abuse cases because of the overriding principle of love—it is simply unloving to a spouse and the kids to stay in an abusive marriage.

While lifetime marriage is clearly God's ideal, it is important to recognize that forgiveness is *always* available. Divorce is not the unpardonable sin. When it is not possible to do the ideal, we must do the next best thing. Even though remarriage is not God's ideal, it may be a realistic accommodation in a less-than-perfect world. We ought to remember the words of 1 John 1:9, "If we confess our sins, He is faithful and righteous to forgive us ours sins and to cleanse us from *all* unrighteousness." Many people have been devastated by divorce and need the loving compassion of Christians—not rules and reasons why they are wrong.

The Truth about Divorce

A great myth in our culture is that divorce makes people happier. *Why should I stay in a difficult marriage,* many people think, *if divorce will make me better off?* Surprisingly, the results show the exact opposite. Consider a few facts about divorce from a major study:[4]

- There is no evidence that divorce makes people happier as a whole.
- Sixty-six percent of unhappily married couples who avoid divorce and stick to their marriage commitment report being happily married within five years.
- Divorce does not decrease symptoms of depression or loneliness, and it does not raise self-esteem.
- The types of problems that lead to divorce *cannot* be sharply distinguished from those that some couples outlast.
- While all marriages face trials, successful marriages are characterized by people who have a commitment to outlast problems and to work on the marriage.

WHY MARRIAGE IS SO IMPORTANT

Not only is marriage important from a biblical standpoint, it is also important for the well-being of society. In fact, there is no factor more vital for the healthy development of a culture than the strength of its marriages. While not everyone should necessarily wed, marriages must be strengthened for the good of society. The Institute for American

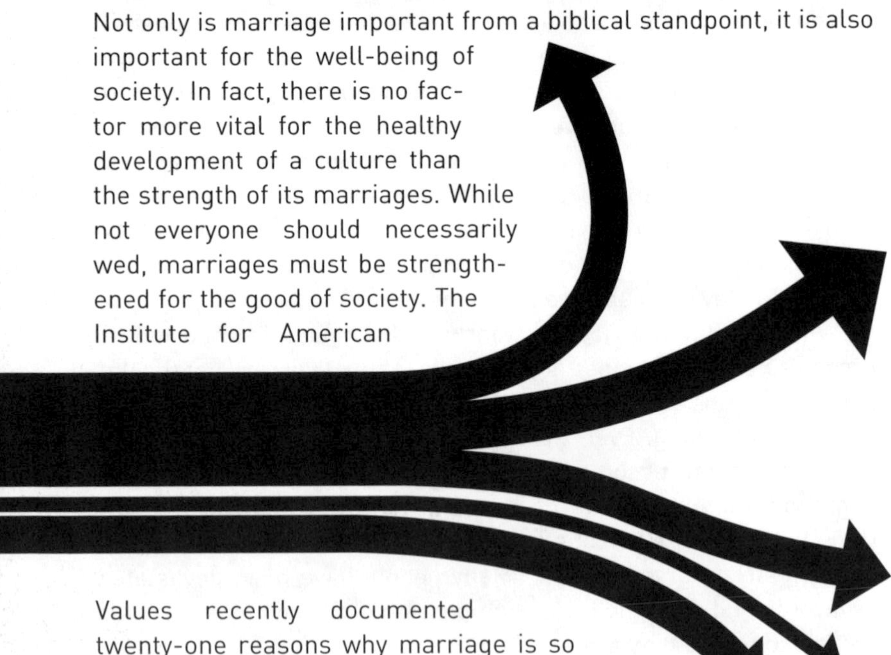

Values recently documented twenty-one reasons why marriage is so important.[5] Here are just a few:

- Married couples build more wealth on average than singles.
- Divorce increases risk-behavior in children.
- Marriage is associated with less alcohol and drug abuse in both teens and adults.
- Married people live longer and healthier lives than singles.
- Married people commit far fewer crimes than singles.

SAME-SEX MARRIAGE

In February 2004, hundreds of same-sex couples rushed to San Francisco to get married. "This is a great thing for us," one lady shouted. "With everyone talking about family, now we can give our daughter a family and no one can take that away from us."

Is same-sex marriage a positive change for society, or is it a negative step? Is marriage *solely* between a man and woman, or can it include same-sex unions? Let's consider some of the primary arguments in support of the legality of same-sex marriage and see whether the traditional understanding of marriage can withstand the onslaught.

"What difference does it make to me?"

Why can't same-sex marriage take place alongside traditional marriage without hurting anyone? Can same-sex marriage be sanctioned without affecting everybody else? To answer this question, consider the following scenario: Imagine you are in a large raft, hoping to get to the other side of the lake safely, when another person insists that he has the right to drill a hole in his side of the raft.[6] When you rightfully object, he charges you with intolerance and bigotry, insisting that you have the right to do what you want on your side but you have no right to interrupt what he does on his. But as water quickly seeps into the raft you realize that, like it or not, what any person does on his side of the raft affects everyone else on board. So, how would the allowance of same-sex marriage hurt everyone? Consider a few implications:

- If same-sex marriage is affirmed, then other relationships could eventually be affirmed as well, such as polygamy and endogamy (union of blood relatives), or marriage to children, or animals, or inanimate objects, and *children are the ones who will be hurt*.
- If same-sex marriage is affirmed, then churches that refuse to perform same-sex weddings will likely lose their tax-exempt status.
- Religious freedom will be lost for those who oppose homosexual behavior. This is already taking place in Canada, where people are fined for speaking against homosexuality in the media, and even from their very own pulpits.

"Homosexuals are being discriminated against."

One of the most frequent arguments given for endorsing same-sex marriage is the claim that homosexuals don't have the same *legal* rights as heterosexuals. In other words, since homosexuals cannot marry each other, they are being lawfully discriminated against by the law. The problem with this claim is that it is simply *false*. Anyone—whether heterosexual or homosexual—can marry in any state in America and receive the rights and benefits of state-sanctioned marriage. All citizens equally share these privileges.

Marriage laws apply equally to all people. What homosexuals want is the right to do something no one has the right to do, namely, marry someone of the same sex. No one can marry a close blood relative, a child, a person who is already married, two people, or a person of the same sex. Denying them this right is not discriminatory; it simply stems from the nature of marriage itself.

"Marriage can be redefined by culture."

Another common justification for same-sex marriage is the claim that marriage is constantly being redefined along with culture. Interestingly, in all cultures of which I am aware, except in a few modern countries, marriage has *always* been between a male and a female. While some have been allowed to marry more than one woman, spouses have always been *male* and *female*. While there have been some variations on the theme of marriage, the core has remained the same—marriage is between a husband and wife.

"Same-sex marriage is a civil rights matter."

Some same-sex marriage advocates have tried to correlate their drive for legal marriage with the civil rights crusades fought by African Americans throughout the past century. Interestingly, the overwhelming majority of African-Americans seem to resent such a move. Why can't same-sex marriage be equated with the civil rights movement? The primary reason is that skin color is not a matter of preference or choice; it is determined *completely* by the genes. But, as we have seen, there has been no genetic link found for homosexual behavior. While people may feel attraction to the same sex, their behavior is chosen. Many people in the past have changed their sexual behavior, but no one has ever shed the color of his skin.[7] To compare skin color and sexual preference is to compare apples and oranges.

"But look at the divorce rate among marriages today!"

Many proponents of same-sex marriage have made a case from the high divorce rate among marriages today. "Don't preach to me about marriage," I heard one young man say. "Just look at all the divorces today." Since there are so many divorces today, shouldn't gay marriage be given a chance? Who are we, since we have been so unfaithful ourselves, to condemn same-sex unions?

To claim that homosexual couples will be more faithful in marriage is quickly contradicted by the facts. While lesbian couples have shown the capacity to sustain long-term bonds, gay males have an infamous record for being promiscuous. In fact, all studies have shown that homosexual males have a need for extramarital outlets. One study of one hundred male homosexual partners who had been together for five years revealed that *none* of them remained exclusively faithful to their partner.[8]

CONCLUSION

Marriage in America is clearly under fire. From the high divorce rate to the challenges of same-sex unions, the institution of marriage is facing challenges like never before. Yet despite the challenges, God still has a purpose and plan for marriage. Marriage is not created by the whim of society, but stems from God's creation. To ignore God's purpose for marriage is to hurt one of the most important instruments God has created for the health of society.

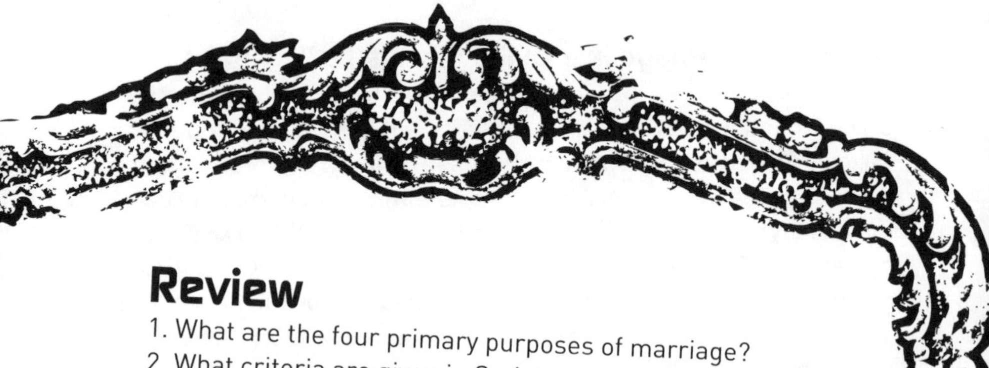

Review

1. What are the four primary purposes of marriage?
2. What criteria are given in Scripture for making divorce permissible?
3. Respond to the claim that, in general, divorce makes people happier.
4. Respond to the following justifications for same-sex unions:
   - *What difference does it make to me?*
   - *Homosexuals are being discriminated against.*
   - *Marriage can be redefined by culture.*
   - *Same-sex marriage is a civil rights matter.*
   - *But look at the divorce rate among marriages today.*

Small Group Discussion

1. Can you think of any other reasons why marriage is so important for a healthy society? In what other ways does marriage strengthen society?
2. How can Christians maintain a commitment to the purpose of marriage without coming across as judgmental and uncaring?

The Morality of War

PURPOSE

To understand the biblical basis for war and learn how to apply principles in the Bible to a particular military conflict

In this chapter you will learn

- To compare and contrast the three primary Christian views of war
- How to use established criteria to determine if a war is just
- How to evaluate the war on terror from a biblical perspective

In March 2003, just eighteen months after the collapse of the Twin Towers in New York, the United States launched a major offensive against Iraq. Eleven days after the start of the war, President Bush gave a speech updating America on the status of *Operation Iraqi Freedom*: "After our nation was attacked on September 11, 2001, America made a decision: We will not wait for our enemies to strike before we act against them. We're not going to permit terrorists and terror states to plot and plan and grow in strength while we do nothing. . . . In every case, by acting today, we are saving countless lives in the future."[1] American involvement was justified by its supporters as a moral obligation to stop the tyrant Saddam Hussein, who was an ally of terrorist groups and a producer of weapons of mass destruction. But many others—unconvinced that Saddam was an imminent threat—felt the war was a diversion from America's real war on terrorism.

Imagine that you are having a class debate over the morality of the war in Iraq. As a Christian student, how would you assess American involvement in the conflict? Did Saddam's use of weapons of mass destruction in the past, his outspoken hatred of the United States, and his financial support of suicide bombers in Israel justify an American invasion of Iraq? Or is this an example of Western military arrogance? Are we policing the world and risking the lives of American troops in a conflict where the United States does not belong? Should a Christian student support his government, or should he protest? On what basis would you make a moral judgment? And how would you incorporate biblical principles into the discussion? As a Christian, how are you to think about war?

As you prepare for your debate presentation, three other Christian students present their positions to the class. They include a Catholic student, a Protestant student, and a Christian whose older brother currently serves in the military. Below are short opening statements that reveal the basic position of each student.

The Christian whose older brother serves in the military

"I believe our generation is growing up in a world much different than previous generations. The world is a very dangerous place, and many leaders of foreign nations will stop at nothing to destroy our freedom and way of life. War is necessary to defend ourselves from tyrants and also to correct many injustices committed against people groups throughout the world. Furthermore, Romans 13 clearly says that the government is to use force, and, since we are citizens of a government, we ought to support our military. I also hold that pre-emptive strikes are necessary when there is an imminent threat."

Protestant Student

"A careful reading of the Bible demonstrates that Jesus would *never* support war. Jesus taught his followers to 'turn the other cheek' and to leave vengeance up to God. He never sanctioned violence for spiritual or governmental means. In fact, in the Sermon on the Mount, Jesus says, 'Blessed are the peacemakers,' which clearly excludes those who support military warfare of any kind. Not only does war contradict the biblical teaching, but it degrades human life. All life is sacred, and it is never acceptable to willingly take the life of another human being. Not only is the war on Iraq unjustified, but all use of violence is wrong as well."

Catholic Student

"I believe that the only wars that can be justified are wars of self-defense. First Timothy 5:8 makes it clear that we are to protect and provide for our families. In the same way, I believe a proper governing authority has the moral right to defend its borders from hostile aggressors. Beyond that I simply cannot support any aggressive use of military force unless it was first initiated by another nation. Therefore, the only justifiable wars are those such as WWII, where allied forces teamed up to defeat the Nazis. Since Iraq did not directly attack the United States, it is debatable whether we had the right to invade them first."

Of the preceding positions, which one do you find yourself agreeing with most? Clearly, since they contradict each other, they can't all be right. But which one best fits with the entire message of the Bible? What should the Christian's attitude be concerning war?

Basically there are three prominent Christian views regarding involvement in war: activism, pacifism, and the just war theory. While the three positions disagree over the role of the Christian in matters of war, *they all agree that the church must never use violence to advance its spiritual mission*.

BIBLICAL ACTIVISM

The first student above holds a position known as *biblical activism*. Biblical activists hold that Christians ought to participate in every war engaged by the government because government is ordained by God. Supporters of this view often cite the numerous biblical examples that clearly indicate that God is the one who institutes government.

The Old Testament

From the very beginning of the Bible, Scripture declares that man was to "be fruitful and multiply, and fill the earth, and subdue it" (Gen. 1:28). Man was to have dominion over the entire earth. Adam was given the crown to reign over the world, and Noah was given the authority to enforce the rule. Since the beginning of time, government was instituted by God to create order in the world and to control disorder.

Even the prophet Daniel declared, "the Most High is ruler over the realm of mankind and bestows it on whomever He wishes" (4:25). The rest of the book of Daniel makes it clear that God controlled the powerful kingdoms of Babylon, Persia, Greece, and Rome. It is clear that God ordains government wherever it is found. Thus, the activists argue that to disobey government is to disobey God Himself. Therefore, a Christian ought to go to war if the government commands it, out of obedience to the Lord.

The New Testament

The New Testament supports the Old Testament message that government is ordained by God. In Matthew 22:21 Jesus said, "Then render to Caesar the things that are Caesar's; and to God the things that are God's." At his trial before Pilate, Jesus further acknowledged the role God plays in establishing government: "You would have no authority over Me, unless it had been given you from above" (John 19:11). In his letter to Titus, Paul says, "Remind them to be subject to rulers, to authorities, to be obedient, to be ready for every good deed" (3:1). And Peter warns followers of Jesus to "Submit yourselves for the Lord's sake to every human institution, whether to a king as the one in authority, or to governors as sent by him for the punishment of evildoers and the praise of those who do right" (1 Pet. 2:13–14).

Romans 13:1–7 is the most extensive discussion in the New Testament regarding the Christian and the role of government. In the first two verses of this passage, Paul says, "Every person is to be in subjection to the governing authorities. For there is no authority except from God, and those which exist are established by God. Therefore whoever resists authority has opposed the ordinance of God; and they who have opposed will receive condemnation upon themselves." Biblical activists conclude from this that Christians are called to support wars initiated by government because God has given authority to the governing authorities.

Criticism of Biblical Activism

There is much truth to be gained from biblical activism. It is unavoidable to conclude that some wars are just and that Christians ought to participate in them. But did the biblical writers really mean that *all* governments throughout the history of the world are just in *all* their actions? Should a Christian uncritically support all actions of human government?

The Bible does teach that there are times when it is right to disobey the government, specifically when its commands are in contradiction with the higher moral laws of God. For example, Shadrach, Meshach, and Abednego clearly disobeyed the governmental authorities when they refused to bow down to an idol (Dan. 3). Daniel refused to obey the law that prohibited him from praying to God (Dan. 6). At the beginning of Exodus the Pharaoh commanded the midwives to kill the newborn male babies of Israel, but they refused and received God's blessing (Exod. 1). Even Jesus' parents disobeyed the government by refusing to turn Jesus over to Herod's henchmen, who were also killing all the newborn male babies (Matt. 2). While government is ordained by God, the government is to be disobeyed when its commands conflict with God's higher laws regarding the protection of innocent human life. While biblical activism makes some important points, it can't account for the full range of biblical data on war. Christians are clearly called to stand up and do the right thing, even if that means taking a stand against the government.

There are also problems with biblical activism outside of the Bible. For one thing, it approves of the credo "Might makes right." In other words, whoever has the most power gets to make the rules about what is right. Therefore, whatever the state does is right, since it has the most power. History will quickly reveal that the state can be deeply corrupt and brutal. If might made right then we would have to approve of the tens of millions of deaths caused by communist governments throughout the twentieth century because they were brought about through the power of the state. The state clearly can be mistaken because there is a higher standard of right and wrong beyond human creation.

PACIFISM

In the examples above, the Protestant student held the position known as *pacifism*. Pacifists hold that it is never justified for a Christian to participate in war. Support for the teachings of pacifism is found in both testaments of the Bible. One of the primary passages cited is the sixth commandment, "You shall not kill" (KJV). At the core of pacifism is the commitment that intentionally taking the life of an innocent person is *always* wrong. This scriptural prohibition is extended to include war, since war involves the deaths of masses of people, including many innocent lives. Since Jesus reaffirmed this Old Testament command when he said, "love your enemies and pray for those who persecute you" (Matt. 5:44), the pacifist believes it is simply un-Christian to be involved in any war that takes the life of an innocent person.

Some pacifists believe that Jesus' teaching, "do not resist an evil person" (Matt. 5:39), applies to individuals as well as national governments. Love, it is argued, would never harm another human being. Even if my homeland is at war, pacifists argue, I must still turn the other cheek regardless of what others do.

According to Isaiah 9:6, Jesus is the "Prince of Peace." He said, "My kingdom is not of this world. If My kingdom were of this world, then My servants would be fighting so that I would not be handed over to the Jews; but as it is, My kingdom is not of this realm" (John 18:36). The weapons are not of this world (2 Cor. 10:4). Jesus' followers are to love their enemies (Matt. 5:44), to overcome evil with good (Rom. 12:21), and to pray for those who persecute them (Matt. 5:44). The right to take life belongs only to God, the author of life (Job 1:21). Human beings simply have no right to kill.

In light of these biblical commands, pacifists hold that participating in war is incompatible with being a believer in Jesus. Pacifists conclude that trusting God and using nonviolent means are the only appropriate measures to stop the progress of evil in the world.

CRITICISM OF PACIFISM

Like biblical activism, there is much truth in pacifism. Some use of force is unjust, and Christians should not be participants in such action. But pacifism also does not completely square with the biblical data. The first problem with pacifism is its contention that humans shall not kill. The sixth commandment is more properly translated as, "You shall not murder." While all murder is killing, *not all killing is murder*. Capital punishment takes a human life, but it is not murder. In fact, in Genesis 9:6 God says, "Whoever sheds man's blood, by man his blood shall be shed, for in the image of God He made man." Killing in self-defense is not murder (Exod. 22:2). Likewise, war in defense of the innocent is not murder either.

Pacifism also does not take into consideration the *entire* message of Christ. While Jesus clearly taught to be at peace with people insofar as it is possible, an appeal to Jesus' example cannot be used to support pacifism under *all* circumstances. Even Jesus himself will be a great military conqueror at the end times according to biblical prophecy.

In assessing Jesus' commands regarding force, the key question is whether he gave an absolute ban of *any* use of force by a Christian authority, or whether he gave a general principle for interpersonal relationships. It seems best to interpret Jesus' teachings about resisting evil as principles in private relationships, not commandments applicable to *every* public situation. For Jesus himself said to cut off the hand and pluck out the eye of those involved in the committing of sexual sin, but he prescribed no such action for the woman caught in adultery or the woman at the well.

A further criticism of pacifism is its prohibition of violence in general. Imagine that a member of your family was being brutally attacked by someone who had broken into your home. He is a crazed killer who has randomly chosen your home, and unless you take immediate action, your family may be dead shortly. You do not have enough time to call 911. So how should you respond? What is most consistent with your Christian commitments? You could try to disarm him without hurting him, but how can you ensure that is possible? What if the only way to stop him is to kill him? It is often argued here that, because you have the higher moral obligation to protect your family than to use nonviolence, force is acceptable. The only way you could truly fulfill the law to love your family would be to resist the attackers, which may include lethal force. In fact, to refuse to use such force may not be the most loving action toward your family. It is sometimes inevitable for an individual and a nation to use force. For reasons like this, many people oppose pacifism and conclude that using force is often the *right* thing to do.

JUST WAR THEORY

While it is true that Jesus' message was primarily pacifist, there is also a recognition in the Bible that the military plays an important role in maintaining a just society. In fact, some have argued that pacifism might even contribute to the spread of evil by refusing to resist its growth. Many quote the famous line, "The only thing necessary for the triumph of evil is for good men to do nothing." Although war is not God's ideal, it is, as we found out with divorce, inevitable in a broken and sinful world. Some of the most biblical saints participated in war. Consider a few:

- *Abraham* fought a battle to resist the kings who were showing unjust national aggression toward his nephew Lot (Gen. 14).

- *Paul* sought protection from the military when he appealed to his Roman citizenship (Acts 22:25–29). On one occasion Paul was protected by a small army of soldiers (Acts 23:23).
- While *Jesus* clearly prohibited his disciples from using force to spread the gospel message, he did instruct them to carry a sword, apparently for protection (Luke 22:36–38).
- Throughout the Old Testament *Israel* was commanded to go to war. God chose physical force as one of the necessary means for his chosen nation to accomplish his purposes (Josh. 6–12; 2 Sam. 5:17–25; 1 Kings 20).
- Two times in the New Testament, *soldiers* were instructed on how to be acceptable to God, and in neither of these occasions were they told to leave the military. Neither Peter nor Jesus say, "Leave the military and sin no more." Yet this is exactly what we would have expected if military service was wrong. Would Jesus have told a prostitute simply not to overcharge her customers?

So how can Jesus' call to live at peace with people be reconciled with the reality of war and the biblical role of the military? While there is truth in both biblical activism and pacifism, there is a third position that squares best with the entirety of the biblical message. The position that has been dominant in the church is known as the *just war theory.* According to this view, Christians should only participate in *some wars*—the *just* ones. Supporters of this view hold that war is justifiable under certain carefully established conditions, more precisely when the response involves self-defense from an unprovoked aggressor. Advocates of the just war theory recognize that war is horrendous but is sometimes necessary to maintain security within one's borders. Only if a military campaign meets *all* of these seven criteria can it be considered just.

1. ***A just cause***—only defensive wars that are a response to aggression can be justified. For example, the attack on Pearl Harbor by the Japanese was just cause for the United States to respond through a declaration of war.
2. ***A just intention***—the intention of the war must be to secure fair peace for all sides involved. It is not justifiable to base a war on desire for economic gain, conquest, or revenge. Wars of genocide clearly contradict this criterion.
3. ***The last resort***—prior to attacking the opposition, all diplomat-

ic efforts must be made to settle the matter peacefully. War can only occur when all negotiations have failed.

4. ***A formal declaration***—war is the role of government, not of individuals. Therefore, a war must be declared by the highest authority and recognized by the appropriate legislative bodies. The element of surprise can still be maintained, but the decision to go to war rests on the governing authorities, not individuals.
5. ***A limited objective***—the purpose must be to secure peace, not to thoroughly destroy a nation's infrastructure. While military capabilities may be destroyed, care must be taken to protect the nation's ability to survive after the war.
6. ***Proportionate means***—the amount of force used must be limited to what is necessary to repel the aggression and ensure future peace. Unnecessary destruction, perhaps by nuclear attack, is arguably ruled out by this criterion.
7. ***Respect noncombatant immunity***—military operations can only target those individuals who are representing their respective governments. Civilians, medics, wounded soldiers, and prisoners of war cannot be objects of attack.

TWO IMPORTANT EXTENSIONS OF THE JUST WAR THEORY

Preemptive Strikes

Many extend the just war theory to also include *preventive strikes*, which is a war begun in anticipation of, rather than in response to, an act of aggression. If an enemy is clearly prepared for an imminent attack and capable of dealing a damaging blow, why should the victim nation have to wait for the attack? A preventive strike can even be seen as a war of self-defense if the indications of danger are clear. There is much debate over this criterion as it applies to the war in Iraq. Did Saddam's use of biological weapons in the past and his desire to obtain new WMD justify the preemptive attack in March, 2003? Or did the United States overstep its rights since it was not attacked first?

The classic example of a justifiable preventive war was the strike by Israel in the 1967 Six-Day War. Israel had very reliable intelligence that their Arab enemies, who were aligned on their border, were aiming to eradicate Israel. Based on their information, it would have been absolutely foolish to wait for the attack. Israel struck their neighbors first and won in one of the most decisive wars in modern history. Yet, the strike clearly had self-defense as the primary goal. If one accepts the just war theory, it may logically follow to accept preemptive strikes as well.

Terrorism

Clearly terrorists do not play by the international rules of engagement. They kill innocent victims, behead captives, and aim to completely destroy the morale of their enemies. As I heard one Middle Eastern terrorist say in a TV interview, "We want the people of the United States to *feel* the terror." So, do the rules of war change when dealing with terrorists?

The first step in answering this question is to define a terrorist. In Romans 13, Paul makes it clear that a criminal is one who internally does evil and threatens the civil peace of a nation. On the other hand, an outside threat to the safety of the state—such as terrorism—is considered an act of war, which is to be handled by the government. Simply put, criminals threaten the state internally; foreign armies threaten the state externally. Terrorists are therefore foreign soldiers who threaten the welfare of the United States.

Evildoers should live in fear of government. Yet, sadly, many foreign nations not only harbor terrorist groups, they support them as well. This makes the terrorists, and the host nations as well, enemies of the United States government, especially when they capture and kill American civilians for military and foreign policy purposes. So what does this mean for the war on terrorism? What follows are a few important considerations.[2]

1. Terrorists should not solely be considered foreign criminals, but *soldiers* intent on destroying the very fabric of American government. They are military targets who must be stopped since they are armed aggressors on the attack.
2. When we fight terrorism it is critical to realize we are talking about *war*, not civilian peacekeeping. In civilian affairs, people are innocent until proven guilty. But in warfare a "trial" of sorts is taken before any action, which includes research, testimonies, and other sorts of fact-finding. Once the research is done, there are no more trials until the defeat of the enemy. And all who aid the enemy are guilty by association.

3. While international diplomacy should be the primary aim of the United States in dealing with terrorism, the truth is that diplomatic efforts have largely failed to convince Middle Eastern governments to side with the United States in fighting terrorism. It needs to be made clear to foreign nations that if they fail to punish terrorism, then they are in complicity with the terrorists and are open to the consequences of allowing hostile military forces within their borders.
4. Exodus 21 makes it clear that punishment must be proportional to the crime. While terrorists do not play by the rules of warfare, this must not be used as an excuse for excessive punishment or humiliation. Excessive responses are not only unjust, but they will fuel the fire of anti-American sentiment.

CONCLUSION

We have seen the variety of positions concerning war within the Christian camp. Although well-meaning Christians vary on the morality of war, the just war theory seems to accord best with the entirety of the biblical message. As long as a military engagement meets the above criteria, it can be considered a just war. Christians can justifiably partake in some wars without fearing that they are contradicting key elements of the faith. In fact, supporting a war can often be the *right* thing to do.

We must never forget that war is a very serious matter *not* to be taken lightly. We should not be flippant about war or eager to support war without truly weighing the cost. War wreaks havoc on human lives and often causes utter destruction. It should truly only be considered when all other options have been exhausted.

Review

1. Define the following three Christian views on war:
   - *Biblical activism*
   - *Pacifism*
   - *Just War*
2. What evidence is given to support biblical activism? What criticisms were raised?
3. What evidence is given to support pacifism? What criticisms were raised?
4. What examples of war are found in the Bible? What criteria must be met for a war to be just?
5. Can a preemptive strike ever be justified according to the just war theory? Why or why not?
6. How might a Christian view the war on terror?

Small Group Discussion

1. How does the war on Iraq fare when compared with the seven criteria for a just war? What about other wars (i.e. the Revolutionary War, the Civil War, the Indian Wars) in American history? What about world history?
2. It's been said that the war on terror is really a war against ideas. What do you think this means? Why are ideas so important in shaping the conflicts in the world?

How to Know God's Will

PURPOSE

To understand the will of God and to learn how to make wise decisions

In this chapter you will learn

- Five principles related to knowing God's will
- That God's will is concerned more with who you are than what you do
- How God gives special guidance to his followers
- How to make wise decisions

One of the most common questions I receive from young people throughout the country is "How can I know the will of God for my life?" To be honest, this question deeply troubled me for many years of my life. What does God want me to do? What if I miss out on God's will? For several difficult years I viewed God's will as being hidden—like an encoded message on a treasure map. I thought my job was to search around while God sent little hints saying things like, "You're getting warmer!"[1] Other times I feared that God's will would only be revealed to me if he took something I loved—such as basketball—away from me. While other people seemed to have a confidence about knowing God's will, I felt no such assurance.

Knowing God's will is no longer a problem for me—and it need not be for you. There are a few biblical principles I have learned about the will of God that have transformed how I make decisions. In the next few pages I would like to share them with you. So, what *is* God's will and how do we know it? It is important to keep in mind that much of God's will has already been revealed in Scripture.

KNOWING GOD'S WILL

Principle #1
God's will is that people be saved.

Genesis 6–9 records the massive flood that wiped out everyone in the world. "Now the earth was corrupt in the sight of God, and the earth was filled with violence. And God looked on the earth, and behold, it was corrupt; for all flesh had corrupted their way upon the earth" (Gen. 6:11–12). Of all the people in the world, Noah was the only person who "walked with God." Even though people had been forewarned about the pending destruction of the world, they ignored the warnings to their own peril.

Writing thousands of years later, the apostle Peter recognized a similar trend infiltrating the church. Then, in Peter's second epistle, he notes that false teachers (whom he compares to dogs returning to their vomit!) deny Jesus' second return. People forget about the flood and assume life will continue at its present pace forever. As a result, people mock God's judgment—just as they did in Noah's day. "But," Peter says, "the day of the Lord will come like a thief, in which the heavens will pass away with a roar and the elements will be destroyed with intense heat, and the earth and its works will be burned up" (2 Pet. 3:10). In other words, just because we may not see God's impending judgment doesn't mean that he can't act. God has made a promise and he intends to keep it. "The Lord is not slack concerning His promise, as some count slackness, but is longsuffering toward us, not *willing* that any should perish but that all should come to repentance" (2 Pet. 3:9 NKJV).

The first aspect of God's will is that, by believing in his son, Jesus Christ, people can be saved. Paul says in 1 Timothy 2:4 that God "desires all men to be saved and to come to the knowledge of the truth." It is God's will that people turn to him in repentance and be saved. If you are stumbling through life trying to know God's will, but have never asked God to forgive your sins, then you are not even in the beginning of God's will. Qualification number one for God's will is your salvation. If you have never committed your life to being a disciple of Jesus, then God has no reason to reveal anything further to you regarding the pattern of your life.

The problem with this criterion is that people today are so quickly offended by sin. Who wants to confront his or her own sin? Rather than taking responsibility for our own lives, we are told that we are victims—victims of our families, genes, or race. But the Bible is clear: "If we say that we have not sinned, we make Him a liar, and His word is not in us" (1 John 1:10). We must be bold enough to admit that we are sinners and in desperate need of God's grace. God's will is that you be saved and that you reach out to others with God's plan of salvation. There is a broken and hurting world that needs God's love and forgiveness—and *you* are the agent to bring his message to that world.

Principle #2
God's will is that people be filled with the Holy Spirit.

Young people often say to me, "I don't understand why God has not revealed to me where I am supposed to go to college or what I am supposed to do with my life. Why doesn't God just reveal his will to me?" Yet many times these students are not even living in the power of the Holy Spirit, which God has already revealed as part of his will. So, what does it mean to live in the *Spirit-filled life*?

At the moment of salvation the Holy Spirit enters the life of *every* Christian. As a result, you have the potential to live a bold life of faith if you are willing to surrender control of your life to him. As we learned in chapter 2, it is the Holy Spirit that convicts us of sin and equips us with the strength to do what is right. It is always amazing to me how few young people truly realize this powerful truth. When I hear Christians say, "God, send me your Spirit," I often wonder why they don't realize that God is already present in their lives! The Holy Spirit is not a force that comes in doses—he is a person who lives within you. As the apostle Paul said, "Do you not know that your body is a temple of the Holy Spirit who is in you, whom you have from God?" (1 Cor. 6:19).

Since we have the Holy Spirit, we also have the power of God in our lives. For Jesus said, "But you will receive power when the Holy Spirit has come upon you; and you shall be my witnesses both in Jerusalem, and in all Judea and Samaria, and even to the remotest part of the earth" (Acts 1:8). In Greek, the original language of the New Testament, the word for power comes from the word for *dynamite*. In other words, Christians are walking around with the power of dynamite within them if they are willing to live in light of that truth.

Peter is an example of someone who possessed miraculous boldness when he was with Christ. He was willing to step out of a boat into stormy water, and he was willing to attack Roman guards at the moment of Jesus' arrest. But when Jesus was gone Peter quickly lost his courage. He denied Christ three times as soon as he realized his neck was on the line. Yet as soon as the Spirit of Christ descended upon him, Peter became a fearless follower of God, facing persecution with the utmost boldness. Where did Peter's strength come from? It came from his being "filled with the Holy Spirit" (Acts 2:4). The same power is available to you if you are willing to surrender control of your life to God through faith.

Principle #3
God's will is that people be pure.

It is pointless for young people (or anybody) to ask God for his *personal* will for their lives when they are not willing to follow his *moral* will. Do you really want to know God's will for your life? Well, here it is: "For this is the will of God, your sanctification; that is, that you abstain from sexual immorality" (1 Thess. 4:3). God's desire for every Christian is that he/she be pure. It is absurd for a young person who is sexually involved to say, "God, reveal your will to me." Since that person is ignoring God's moral will, why should he reveal some further will?

Am I saying you can't hold hands with your boyfriend or girlfriend? That is not the point. Am I saying you can't kiss? That's not the point, either. I am frequently asked by high school students, "How far is too far?" Yet the Bible says, "Whatever is true, whatever is honorable, whatever is right, whatever is pure, whatever is lovely, whatever is of good repute, if there is any excellence and if anything worthy of praise, let your mind dwell on these things" (Phil. 4:8). You can be blessed by God only so far as what you are doing is true, honorable, right, and pure. When you are controlled by lust rather than the Spirit of God, you are no longer in God's will.

Being pure also involves controlling your body and your eyes. God's will is "that each of you know how to possess his own vessel in sanctification and honor" (1 Thess. 4:4). This means controlling what you watch with your eyes and the way you dress.

Principle #4
God's will is that people submit to the proper authorities.

Few people realize that the first of the Ten Commandments concerning interpersonal relationships is the fifth: *Honor your father and mother*. The first four commandments have to do with the relationship between people and God, and the last six have to do with the relationship between people. And honoring our parents is listed before the commands not to lie, murder, or even steal! In fact, God was so serious about people obeying their parents that young people were killed during the time of the Old Testament for dishonoring their parents. While we can be thankful that this is not the case anymore, this does give us some insight into how highly God values respect for parents. *God's will is simple: Obey your parents and the proper authorities.*

First Peter 2:18 says, "Be submissive to your masters [parents, teachers, coaches] with all respect. . . ." You might be thinking, *But Sean, you don't know my parents.* But the verse continues, ". . . not only for those who are good and gentle, but also to those who are *unreasonable*." Do you have unreasonable parents? What are you to do? Submit with respect. Of course, if an authority asks you to do something that goes against God's higher command, then obey God. But these times are few and far between.

Principle #5–
God's will is that people suffer for doing what is right.

Being a Christian is not always easy. If you really want to stand up for what is right you *will be persecuted*—period. Anyone who tries to tell you differently is watering down the message of Christ. This is why the apostle Peter wrote, "For it is better, if God should will it so, that you suffer for doing what is right rather than for doing what is wrong" (1 Pet. 3:17). You might get made fun of for not drinking or for not going to see a certain movie. You might be shunned by your family for choosing to follow Christ. And you may get rejected for sharing your faith. *But God's will is simple: Trust him even when we suffer for doing what is right.*

If you are a Christian filled with the Holy Spirit, you will suffer for doing what is right. If you are living a godly life in an ungodly world, you will suffer. The apostle Paul wrote, "Indeed, all who desire to live godly in Christ Jesus will be persecuted" (2 Tim. 3:12). You might be thinking, *But I don't suffer any persecution.* Then possibly you are not truly standing up for what is right. If you do suffer, then rejoice: "If you are insulted because of the name of Christ, you are blessed, for the Spirit of glory and of God rests on you" (1 Pet. 4:14 NIV).

GOD'S WILL IS YOU!

God's will is that you be saved, be filled with the Holy Spirit, be pure, submit to the proper authorities, and that you trust God when you suffer. The Bible makes it very clear that this is God's will for your life. Yet you might be thinking, *What about God's* specific *will for my life? I thought you were going to tell me how to find out where I should go to college or how to find my spouse!*

Well, if that's what you are looking for, then here is the final principle: If you have truly followed the first five principles then you are free to make choices based on your desires. And if you are living a godly life, God will give you the right desires. This is why the psalmist says, "Delight yourself in the LORD; and He will give you the desires of your heart" (Ps. 37:4).

In other words, if we first give control of our lives to God, then we have the freedom to make choices because he is truly guiding our lives. You see, God's will is not so much about what you do, *but about who you are*. God's will is not so much about where you go to college, but about the type of student you are. God's will is not so much about who you date, but how you treat people of the opposite sex. God has dignified you with the freedom of making choices.

Dr. John MacArthur explains the essence of God's will: "You see, the will of God is not primarily a place. The will of God is not, first of all, for you to go there or work here. The will of God concerns you as a person. If you are the right you, you can follow your desires and you will fulfill His will."[2]

So here's the take-home principle: *Don't wait around for God's special personalized directive. Get involved NOW!* Get involved in a youth group, missions, Bible club, or student outreach. Develop convictions about what you believe and why you believe it. When you begin moving, God can steer you in the direction he wants you to go. This is why the writer of Proverbs said, "The mind of man plans his way, but the LORD directs his steps" (16:9).

WHAT ABOUT GOD'S SPECIFIC PLAN FOR MY LIFE?

I know God's *specific* will for your life. When I tell this to my students, they often think this means I've received a special word from God, and that I'm about to tell them where they should go to college or who they will someday marry. But their eyes sometimes convey their disappointment when I share with them the five principles you just read. "But what about *my* life?" they often say. "How can I know *specifically* what God wants me to do with my life?"

As a high school senior, this question was at the forefront of my wife's mind. She greatly desired to go to Biola University where I was attending, but the finances were overwhelming. While some in her family encouraged her to attend a state school, she knew she would only be truly happy at a Christian university. She prayed eagerly that God would direct her to a place that she could afford. Although disappointed that the doors were closed to attend Biola (because of finances), she decided to go to Vanguard University. There she received both an academic and basketball scholarship.

Stephanie's desire was to go in one direction, but the Lord directed her steps somewhere else. And in the end, she loved every aspect of being at Vanguard. Would she have been out of God's will to still attend Biola or a state school? No, because what we have learned in this chapter is that God's will involves *who* she is more than *what* she does. God would have been with her no matter where she chose to attend college.

So, how are you to make godly decisions? Before I share with you biblical principles on how to make specific decisions for your life, let me share with you two important concepts about how God gives guidance.[3]

The Spirit Leads Us with the Strength to Make Right Choices.

It is amazing to me how often I hear people say, "I am feeling led by God to do such and such." I can't help but wonder how they know this. As far as I know, there is not a single instance in the Bible where it is taught that God speaks to us through our feelings. Within the Christian subculture it is common for people to claim that God leads them through their feelings. I would be cautious in using this particular language because I find such a claim difficult to support with Scripture. Proverbs 3:5 says, "Trust in the LORD with all your heart and do not lean on your own understanding." We should not trust our feelings, for our feelings can so easily lead us astray. So, what *does* it mean to be "led by the Spirit"?

Romans 8:12–14 says, "So then, brethren, we are under obligation, not to the flesh, to live according to the flesh—for if you are living according to the flesh, you must die; but if by the Spirit you are putting to death the deeds of the body, you will live. For *all who are being led by the Spirit of God*, these are sons of God." Being led by the Spirit refers not to individual guidance, but strength to live a righteous life—to stand up for what is right. The Spirit leads us by convicting us of sin and empowering us to make right choices.

God Opens Doors, Yet Gives Us the Freedom to Walk Through Them.

The apostle Paul was given some open doors for ministry: "But I will remain in Ephesus until Pentecost; for a wide door for effective service has opened to me, and there are many adversaries" (1 Cor. 16:8–9). In this instance Paul was given an open door and he decided to follow it.

Yet in other instances Paul actually ignores open doors. "Now when I [Paul] came to Troas for the gospel of Christ and when a door was opened for me in the Lord, I had no rest for my spirit, not finding Titus my brother; but taking my leave of them, I went on to Macedonia" (2 Cor. 2:12–13). And again in Acts 16:26–28 Paul ignores an open door: "And suddenly there came a great earthquake, so that the foundations of the prison house were shaken; and immediately all the doors were opened, and everyone's chains were unfastened. When the jailer awoke and saw the prison doors opened, he drew his sword and was about to kill himself, supposing that the prisoners had escaped. But Paul cried out with a loud voice, saying, 'Do not harm yourself, for we are all here!'" (Acts 16:26–28). Even Paul viewed open doors as opportunities that he had the choice to act on or ignore rather than some secret revelation of God's will.

MAKING CHOICES THROUGH WISDOM

We have seen that God is far more concerned with who we are than what we do. So, the question still remains "How are we to make choices about an important decision in life?" The Bible teaches that we are to *seek wisdom*. In fact, we are commanded to seek wisdom with all we have: "How much better it is to get wisdom than gold! And to get understanding is to be chosen above silver" (Prov. 16:16).

So, how do we get wisdom? James 1:5 tells us to ask God for wisdom, "But if any of you lacks wisdom, let him ask of God, who gives to all generously and without reproach, and it will be given to him." Even Solomon, the wisest man in history, asked for wisdom: "Give me now wisdom and knowledge, that I may go out and come in before this people; for who can rule this great people of Yours?" (2 Chron. 1:10). We also get wisdom from reading God's Word, seeking godly advice from our elders, and from our experience. Proverbs 13:10 says, "But wisdom is with those who receive counsel." If you are willing to seek godly wisdom, then God will shape your desires and ultimately guide your steps.

CONCLUSION

God's will is that you be saved, be filled with the Holy Spirit, be pure, submit to the proper authorities, and that you trust God when you suffer. Yet the most important thing about God's will is YOU! God's will does not so much involve what you do but who you are. God's will is that you be a godly person who stands up for what is right. And when you need to make important decisions, seek wisdom through prayer, wise counsel, and God's Word.

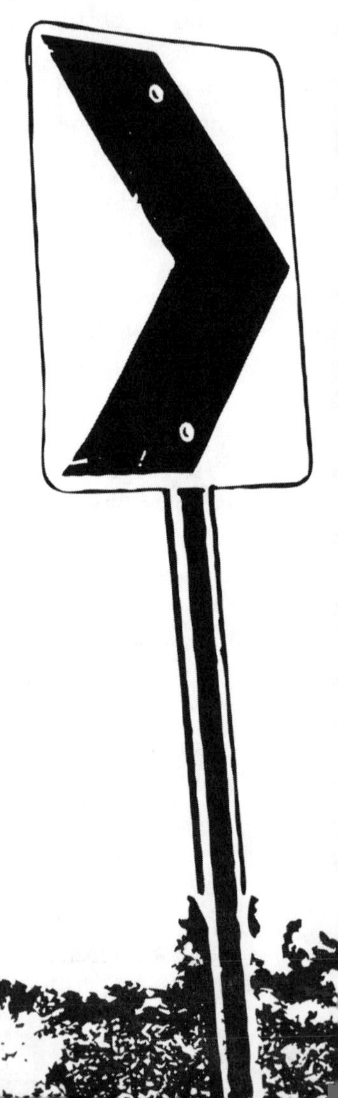

1. What is God's will regarding salvation?
2. What does it mean to be "filled with the Holy Spirit"?
3. How does God desire his people to be pure?
4. What is God's will regarding his followers and proper authorities?
5. Who will suffer according to God's will? Why?
6. What does it mean that God's will is you?
7. Describe how God gives guidance in the Scriptures.
8. How are we to make difficult decisions?

Small Group Discussion

1. Read 1 Corinthians 7:1–16 carefully. What does this passage reveal about God's will for relationships? Is this passage more concerned with finding God's will for who you are to marry, or being the right type of spouse? Or both?
2. In what ways do you think the will of God is misunderstood in many Christian circles today? Why is it so hard for people to focus on the will of God as revealed in Scripture?

Recommended Resources

The following are recommended reading for further inquiry on contemporary ethical issues and moral truth:

Moral Absolutes

Francis J. Beckwith & Gregory Koukl, *Relativism: Feet Firmly Planted in Thin Air* (Grand Rapids, MI: Baker Books, 1998).

Norman L. Geisler, *Christian Ethics: Options and Issues* (Grand Rapids, MI: Baker Books, 1989).

Paul Copan, *True for You, but Not for Me: Deflating the Slogans That Leave Christians Speechless* (Minneapolis, MN: Bethany House Publishers, 1998).

C. S. Lewis, *The Abolition of Man* (San Francisco, HarperSanFrancisco: 2001).

J. Budzizewski, *Written on the Heart: The Case for Natural Law* (Downers Grove, Ill.: InterVarsity Press, 1997).

Contemporary Moral Issues

Francis J. Beckwith, *Do the Right Thing: Readings in Applied Ethics and Social Philosophy* (Florence, KY: Wadsworth Publishing, 2001).

Kerby Anderson, *Christian Ethics in Plain Language* (Nashville, TN: 2005).

Scott B. Rae, *Moral Choices* (Grand Rapids, MI: 2000).

Peter Kreeft, *Making Choices* (Cincinnati, OH: Servant Books, 1990).

Recommended Web Sites on Ethical Issues

Stand to Reason: www.str.org
Leadership University: www.leaderu.com
Probe Ministry: www.probe.org
The Center for Bioethics & Human Dignity: www.cbhd.org

Notes

Chapter 1

1. Pamela Paul, "The Power of Uplift," *Time* (January 17, 2005), A46–48.
2. Jimmy Carter, *Living Faith* (New York: Times Books, 1996), 161.
3. Heather Farish, "The Whole Story on Sex," press release (Washington, D.C.: Family Research Council; March 29, 2001).
4. "Abortion and Breast Cancer Linked in Report," *World* (October 26, 1996), 18.
5. "Study: Post-abortive Women Suffer," *Citizen* (February 2005), 8.
6. Thomas Schmidt, *Straight and Narrow?* (Downers Grove, Ill.: InterVarsity Press, 1995), 121.

Chapter 2

1. Sarah Childress and Dirk Johnson, "The Hot Sound of Hate," *Newsweek* (November 29, 2004).

Chapter 3

1. Josh McDowell and Thomas Williams, *In Search of Certainty* (Wheaton, Ill.: Tyndale, 2003).
2. C. S. Lewis, *Mere Christianity* (New York: Macmillan, 1960), 58.
3. J. P. Moreland and William Lane Craig, *Philosophical Foundations for a Christian Worldview* (Downers Grove, Ill.: InterVarsity Press, 2003), 130–31.
4. I am grateful to Peter Kreeft for his insights, from his book *Making Choices* (Cincinnati, Ohio: Servant Books, 1990), 9–11.
5. I am indebted to Gregory Koukl, president of *Stand to Reason*, for his insights on this distinction.
6. Lewis, *Mere Christianity*, 19–20.
7. Kreeft, *Making Choices*, 45.
8. Paul Copan, *True for You, but Not for Me* (Minneapolis, Minn.: Bethany House Publishers, 1998), 23.
9. McDowell and Williams, *In Search of Certainty*.

Chapter 4

1. Allen Bloom, *The Closing of the American Mind* (New York:

Simon and Schuster, 1987), 25.

2. This illustration was used by Paul Copan, *True for You, but Not for Me* (Minneapolis, Minn.: Bethany House, 1998), 17.
3. J. P. Moreland, *Love Your God with All Your Mind* (Colorado Springs, Colo.: NavPress, 1997), 153.
4. Peter Kreeft, *Making Choices* (Cincinnati, Ohio: St. Anthony Messenger Press, 1990), 37.
5. Norman L. Geisler, *Baker Encyclopedia of Christian Apologetics* (Grand Rapids: Baker Books, 1999), 502.
6. Francis J. Beckwith, "Why I Am Not a Moral Relativist," *Why I Am a Christian: Leading Thinkers Explain Why They Believe*, Norman L. Geisler and Paul K. Hoffman, eds. (Grand Rapids: Baker, 2001), 24.
7. For further research on God's existence, see Norman Geisler and Joseph Holden, *Living Loud* (Nashville: Broadman & Holman, 2002); and for a more advanced study, consider Norman Geisler and Frank Turek, *I Don't Have Enough Faith to Be an Atheist* (Wheaton, Ill.: Crossway Books, 2004).
8. Mother Theresa, "We Must Give Until It Hurts," *World* (February 12, 1994), 22–24.
9. Francis J. Beckwith, "Do the Right Thing: Readings in Applied Ethics and Social Philosophy," 2nd ed. (Belmont, Calif.: Wadsworth, 2002), xii.
10. Gregory Koukl, "Homosexuality: Giving Your Point of View," www.str.org/free/commentaries/homosexuality/homosex1.htm, (downloaded July 21, 2004).

Chapter 5

1. Lorraine Ali and Julie Scelfo, "Choosing Virginity," *Newsweek* (December 9, 2002), 61–66.
2. See Josh McDowell, *Right from Wrong* (Dallas, Tex.: Word Publishing, 1994), 147–66.
3. Peter Kreeft, *Making Choices* (Cincinnati, Ohio: St. Anthony Messenger Press, 1990), 101.
4. *Seventeen*, "Sex and Body" (January 2000).
5. Ronald O. Valdiserri, M.D., speaking to the Subcommittee on Health and Environment about cervical cancer, House Committee on Commerce, *Congressional Record* (March 16, 1999), 18–22.
6. Medical Institute for Sexual Health, "Listing of Sexually Transmitted Diseases" (1994); www.wcpc.org/sexuality/std.html.

7. Valdiserri, speech, 3.
8. William Archer III, M.D., *Sexual Health Update Newsletter* 7:3 (Fall 1999).
9. National Institutes of Health Consensus Development Program, "Cervical Cancer," *Consensus Development Statements* 14:1 (April 1–3, 1996); www.odp.od.nih.gov/consensus/cons/102/102_intro.htm
10. Ibid.
11. "Safe Sex?" (Austin, Tex.: The Medical Institute, 1999), documented slide presentation.
12. Josh McDowell, *Why True Love Waits* (Wheaton, Ill.: Tyndale, 2002), 321.
13. Ibid., 325.
14. Fred R. Berger, "Pornography, Sex, and Censorship," *Do the Right Thing*, Francis J. Beckwith, ed. (Belmont, Calif.: Wadsworth, 2002), 589.
15. William R. Mattox Jr., "Aha! Call It the Revenge of the Church Ladies," *USA Today* (February 11, 1999), 15A.
16. Acts 15:20; 1 Corinthians 6:9, 13; Galatians 5:19; 1 Thessalonians 4:3.
17. Walter Trobisch, *I Loved a Girl* (New York: Harper & Row, 1975), 8.
18. *National Review* (December 31, 1995).
19. Sonya Jason, "Scourge of the Valley Pornography Undermines Decent Society," *Daily News* (Los Angeles, Calif.: May 23, 2004).
20. Robertson McQuilkin, *An Introduction to Biblical Ethics* (Wheaton, Ill.: Tyndale, 1995), 221.
21. J. Kerby Anderson, *Moral Dilemmas* (Nashville: Word, 1998), 148.
22. Robert H. Bork, *Slouching Towards Gomorrah: Modern Liberalism and American Decline* (New York: HarperCollins, 1996).
23. "Medically Speaking—Oral Sex and STDs," Sexual Health Update (The Medical Institute, Fall 2003).
24. Ibid.
25. 1 Corinthians 6:18; 1 Peter 5:9.
26. As quoted in Scott B. Rae, *Moral Choices* (Grand Rapids: Zondervan, 2000), 241.

Chapter 6

1. Laura D'Angelo, "'E' is for Empty: Daniel's Story," the National Institute for Drug Abuse, www.teens.drugabuse.

gov/stories/story_xtc1.asp (downloaded January 10, 2005).
2. Ibid.
3. As cited in Kerby Anderson, *Moral Dilemmas* (Nashville: Word Publishing, 1998), 113.
4. "Marijuana: Facts Parents Need to Know," the National Institute for Drug Abuse, www.nida.nih.gov/marijBroch/parentpg11-12N.html#Harmful (downloaded March 25, 2005).
5. "Ecstasy," the National Institute for Drug Abuse, www.teens.drugabuse.gov/facts/facts_xtc2.asp (downloaded January 10, 2005).

Chapter 7

1. Kerby Anderson, *Moral Dilemmas* (Nashville: Word Publishing, 1998), 4–5.
2. John Ankerberg and John Weldon, *The Facts on Abortion* (Eugene, Ore.: Harvest House Publishers, 1995), 6–10.
3. The timeline was adapted from "A Baby's First Months," a booklet made available by Tennessee Right to Life (Nashville) www.tnrtl.org.
4. This three-part argument is developed by Gregory Koukl, *Precious Unborn Human Persons* (San Pedro, Calif.: Stand to Reason Press), 16–23.
5. Ibid., 16.
6. Ibid., 22.
7. Ronald Reagan, *Abortion and the Conscience of the Nation* (Nashville: Nelson, 1984), 21, as quoted in Robertson McQuilkin, *Biblical Ethics* (Wheaton, Ill.: Tyndale, 1989), 315.
8. Scott B. Rae, *Moral Choices* (Grand Rapids: Zondervan, 2000), 139.
9. Richard Werner, "Abortion: The Moral Status of the Unborn," *Social Theory and Practice* 4 (Spring 1975), 202.
10. *Merriam-Webster's Collegiate Dictionary*, 10th ed. (Springfield, Mass.: Merriam-Webster, 1998).
11. Ankerberg and Weldon, *The Facts on Abortion*, 17.

12. This acronym is from Stephen Schwarz, *The Moral Question of Abortion* (Chicago: Loyola University Press, 1990), 15.
13. Scott Klusendorf, *Pro-Life 101* (Signal Hill, Calif.: Stand to Reason Press, 2002).
14. Rae, *Moral Choices*, 135.
15. Gwendolyn Mitchell Diaz, *Sticking Up for What Is Right* (Colorado Springs, Colo.: NavPress, 2002), 111.
16. Reagan, *Abortion and the Conscience of the Nation*, 38.

Chapter 8

1. Jude 7; 2 Peter 2:7–10.
2. J. S. Feinberg, P. D. Feinberg, *Ethics for a Brave New World* (Wheaton, Ill.: Crossway Books, 1996, c1993).
3. Mark 7:18; Acts 10:12.
4. Romans 1:26–27; 1 Corinthians 6:9; 1 Timothy 1:10; Jude 7.
5. James Dobson, *Bringing up Boys* (Wheaton, Ill.: Tyndale, 2001), 113–29.
6. See M. King and E. MacDonald, "Homosexuals Who Are Twins: A Study of Forty-Six Probands" *British Journal of Psychiatry* 160 (1992), 407–409; and Joe Dallas, *Desires in Conflict* (Eugene, Ore.: Harvest House, 1991), 90.
7. David Gelman, "Born or Bred?" *Newsweek* (February 24, 1992), 46.
8. John Ankerberg and John Weldon, *The Facts on Homosexuality* (Eugene, Ore.: Harvest House, 1994), 14–15.
9. Ibid.
10. J. Crewdson, "Study on 'Gay Gene' Challenged," *Chicago Tribune* (June 25, 1995), 1, 10–11.
11. Stanton L. Jones and Mark A. Yarhouse, "The Use, Misuse, and Abuse of Science," *Homosexuality, Science and the "Plain Sense" of Scripture*, David L. Balch, ed. (Grand Rapids: Eerdmans, 2000), 94–95.
12. This point was made by Gwendolyn Mitchell Diaz in *Sticking up for What Is Right: Answers to the Moral Dilemmas Teenagers Face* (Colorado Springs, Colo.: NavPress, 2002), 94–95.
13. Thomas E Schmidt, *Straight and Narrow?* (Downers Grove, Ill.: InterVarsity Press, 1995), 110–20.

14. My thanks to Gregory Koukl for his insights, from his article, "Doing What Comes Naturally" *Solid Ground* (May/June 2002), 1–2.
15. Ibid., 1.
16. Charles Colson, *Answers to Your Kids' Questions* (Wheaton, Ill.: Tyndale, 2000), 116.

Chapter 9

1. Julie Scelfo, "Happy Divorce," *Newsweek* (December 6, 2004), 42.
2. *Merriam-Webster's Collegiate Dictionary*, 10th ed. (Springfield, Mass.: Merriam-Webster, 1998).
3. John S. Feinberg and Paul D. Feinberg, *Ethics for a Brave New World* (Wheaton, Ill.: Crossway Books, 1996), 329.
4. "Does Divorce Make People Happy?," Institute for American Values (New York, 2002). This report was written by a team of scholars headed up by Linda J. Waite, www.americanvalues.org.
5. "Why Marriage Matters: Twenty-One Conclusions from the Social Sciences," Institute for American Values (New York, 2002), www.americanvalues.org.
6. Erwin W. Lutzer, *The Truth about Same-Sex Marriage* (Chicago, Ill.: Moody Press, 2004), 25–26.
7. Ibid., 79–80.
8. Ibid., 85.

Chapter 10

1. "President Updates America on Operations Liberty Shield and Iraqi Freedom," www.whitehouse.gov/news/releases/2003/03/20030331-4.html (March 31, 2003).
2. For a more in-depth article on the war on terror, see "Terrorism" by Kerby Anderson, www.leaderu.com/orgs/probe/docs/terror.html#.

Chapter 11

1. Much of this chapter is adapted from John MacArthur Jr., *Found: God's Will* (Colorado Springs, Colo.: Chariot Victor, 1977).
2. Ibid., 59.
3. My thanks to Gregory Koukl of Stand to Reason for his insights regarding God's will. For further reference see his CD series, "Decision Making and the Will of God," available at www.str.org.